DAVID L. MILLER

THE NEW POLYTHEISM

Rebirth of the Gods and Goddesses

SPRING PUBLICATIONS
THOMPSON, CONN.

Published by Spring Publications
Thompson, Conn.
www.springpublications.com

First published in 1974 by Harper & Row, New York

Third, revised edition 2021 (v. 3.1)

Library of Congress Control Number: 2021912990

ISBN: 978-0-88214-939-4

For my mother and father

CONTENTS

PREFACE

A Letter by HENRY CORBIN

February 9, 1978
Paris

Dear Colleague and Friend,

On returning from Tehran two weeks ago, I had the great pleasure of finding the copy of your book *The New Polytheism* with its friendly dedication. Not only do I thank you for it with all my heart, but I can assure you that I immediately began to read it and that it was a passionate and enthusiastic reading.

I cannot say everything in a letter. We shall have to speak more at our leisure at Eranos, and that could take us far. Nonetheless, I do want to tell you right now how I am struck by the convergence of our research, even though we do not express ourselves altogether in the same vocabulary. This is just, however, since our points of departure were different, even though our points of arrival are remarkably near to each other...

What I mean is that I have been guided by the way in which the great theosophist Ibn 'Arabī and his School meditated on *tawhīd* ("the Attestation of the One") to staggering heights. There is a theological *tawhīd*, which is the profession of exoteric monotheistic faith, i.e., "There is no God but God." And there is an esoteric ontological *tawhīd* that states: "There is no Being but God." The catastrophe results (already long ago) from confusing Being [*Être*] (Latin *esse*, Arabic *wujūd*) with a being [*Étant*] (Latin *ens*, Arabic *mawjūd*).

If, in effect, God is solely Being [*Être*], then he could not himself properly be a being or an *ens* [*Étant*], not even a "Supreme Being" (*ens supremum*). By confusing Being with a supreme being (*ens supremum*), that is, by making of *Esse* an *ens supremum*, monotheism perishes in its triumph. It elevates an idol just at the point where it denounces such in a polytheism it poorly understands.

Only a negative theology (apophatic) is able to encompass by indirection the mystery of Being (*Esse*). But official monotheism never had much love for negative theology. In so far as Being [*Être*] brings each existent [*étant*] into being, it must itself be beyond all existence [*Étant*]. It is impossible to express this mystery of Being that brings each being into being, that is, this mystery of the One that brings each being into being as an existent [*étant*]. Its unity (*unitude*) is $1 \times 1 \times 1 \times 1$, *etc.*, while the multiple unity of beings [*étants*] is represented by $1 + 1 + 1 + 1$, *etc.* To confuse Being with a being is the metaphysical catastrophe. It is the "death of Being" to confuse the unity of Being (*Esse*) with a pseudo-unity of beings (*ens*), which is essentially multiple.

It is precisely this confusion that monotheism has committed, a confusion between the *Theotēs* (Divinity) and the *theoi* (gods). A unique *Theotēs* is not to be confused with a unique theos, any more than unique Being is to be confused with a unique being. There can be only one *Theotēs* just as Being (*Esse*) is unique. Were this not the case, we would not be able even to speak of the gods in the plural. The predicate precedes the subject, which is why Being is antecedent to being [*étant*], and why Divinity [*Theotēs*] precedes both God [*theos*] and the gods [*theoi*]. A unique God as a supreme being (*ens supremum*) will always follow upon the Divinity that one attributes to it.

By confusing the uniqueness of Divinity (*Theotēs*) with a singular God (*theos*) that excludes all other gods (*theoi*), unique Being with a singular being, monotheistic theology has itself prepared the way for precisely what your book shows so well, "the death of God," just as the confusion between Being and beings entails the "death of Being," leaving a place only for a totalitarian sense of the existent [*étant*].

In return, the unity of *Theotēs* entails, conditions, and guarantees the plurality of the *theoi* (gods), just as the unity of Being entails and conditions the plurality of beings. The *Non Deus nisi Deus* [There is no God but God) becomes *Non Deus nisi Dii* ["There is no God without gods"). (The expression *Ilāh al-Āliha*, "God of Gods," occurs frequently in Sohrawardī.) It is in the very nature of the *Theotēs* (*deitas abscondita*) to be revealed and made manifest by the plurality of its theophanies, in an unlimited number of theophanic forms. Theomonism bears within itself the rebirth of the gods as theophames of the *Theotēs*, and this renaissance conditions the rebirth of religious individuality, about which each can say, and can say nothing other than: *Talem eum vidi qualem capere potui* [I am able to grasp such as I have seen]. This is the gnostic formulation *par excellence*. You said it in your book: "God has died of a long disease called 'monotheism.'" But the God of the gnostics can never die because he is himself [the place of] the renaissance of gods and goddesses.

This is why, dear friend, my vocabulary differs a bit from yours. The theogony and theology of our Greek masters has been degraded into frivolity by secular art (e.g., Renaissance paintings). But since my research has proceeded from the Iranian Sohrawardī and from Ibn 'Arabī of Andalusia, I speak always of the multitude of theophanies and of theophanic forms. The uniquely Divine (*Theotēs*) aspires to be revealed and can only be revealed in multiple theophanies. Each one is autonomous, different from the other, each quite close to being a hypostasis, yet at the same time the totality of *Theotēs* is in each theophanic form.

Moreover, rather than polytheism, I have spoken often of mystical *kathenotheism*. The *kath'hena* seems to me to be the category that is essential for the pluralism of theophanic forms. These are like the *Dii-Angeli* of Proclus, and I believe that my theophanic *kathenotheism* is allied with your "polytheism" in the sense that it is like a monadology that frees us from the totalitarian block of monotheism and from its secular forms.

I believe that our guide *par excellence* on this road remains the great and so long misunderstood Proclus. His work speaks of the *henad* or *henads*, and the henads monadizing the monads are on a level with Ibn 'Arabī's cosmology of Divine Names. The theophanic and cosmogonic function of the twelve great gods in Proclus, the twelve Imāms in Shi'ite neoplatonism, the ten Sephiroth in the Kabbala—it is the One [*l'Unique*] himself who attests to these multiplicities of ones [*uniques*]. Compare also the hypercosmic and intracosmic gods and the *Dii-Angeli* of Proclus. But few know of this, often only the esotericists of the Religions of the Book.

Israel was able to serve only "its" God, and could proclaim the unity of only "its" God (which theophanically is the sixth Sephiroth according to the Kabbalists). Each of us, as well, has to recognize "his" God, the one to which he [is able to] respond. I believe our researches open the way, of necessity, to angelology (that of a Proclus, that of the Kabbala), which will be reborn with increasing potency. The Angel is the Face that our God takes for us, and each of us finds his God only when he recognizes that Face. The service that we can render others is to help them encounter that Face about which they will be able to say: *Talem eum vidi qualem capere potui* [I am able to grasp such as I have seen].

I am troubled, dear friend, by the proportions this letter is taking. But I believe it is useful and necessary that I recapitulate

for you my way of seeing and that I explain to you why I experience its convergence with your perspective. But let us understand clearly that for yet some time we shall be few in number
and that we shall have to take refuge behind the veil of a certain
esotericism.

You said very well that this work is a matter neither of alle-
gorism nor of historicism. I agree completely. That is why, guided
by my Iranian philosophers, I have for many years endeavored
to restore both logically and gnoseologically a mediating and
intermediary world which I call *mundus imaginalis* (Arabic *ʿālam
al-mithāl*). This is an imaginal world not to be confused with the
imaginary. Such has been my great meeting ground with our
friend, James Hillman, and I congratulate you for having shown
so well in your book the originality and courage of his position.
If Iranian philosophers have considered the *mundus imaginalis*
indispensable for placing the visions of prophets and mystics,
this is because it is there that they "take place," and deprived of
this imaginal world they no longer "take place." I believe that this
imaginal world is the locus of the "rebirth of the gods," those of
Greek theogony, as well as of Celtic theogony, which with those of
the Greeks and Iranians, are the closest to our consciousness.

This is why I attentively read and re-read the statement of
your theses in Chapter Four. Above all, these two: (1) "A polytheistic theology will be Gnostic, but in the manner of the secret
knowledge of Hermes"; (2) "It will be a theology of spirit (with reference to Berdyaev), but in the manner of the multicolored butterfly released from the cocoon that is the dwelling of the worm."
Agreed, agreed! We shall come back to all this at Eranos.

Some of my latest works relate especially to your book: (1)
"Le Paradoxe du monothéisme," *Eranos 1976* (but I have not yet
received the proofs); (2) "Necessité de l'angelologie," about sev-
enty pages, which will appear very soon in one of the *Cahiers de*

l'Hermetisme and I will send it to you right away; (3) "De la théol-
ogie apophatique comme antidote du nihilisme," a long lecture
given in Tehran on the occasion of a colloquium in October 1977,
the publication of which has not yet appeared.[1] Does Syracuse
University have my books? If not, I must find some copies for you.
I call your attention to my work on Ibn 'Arabī translated into English as *Creative Imagination in the Sufism of Ibn 'Arabī* (Princeton
University Press). It contains numerous references to *kathenotheism,* but these are not noted in the English index. In the event
that this interests you, I could get you a copy of the second
French edition.

We have formed a small group of free academics (Gilbert
Durand, Jean Brun, Jean Servier, and others) under the name of
The University of St. John of Jerusalem.[2] We investigate these sorts
of questions concerning the Religions of the Book. There is one
meeting a year, and we publish the proceedings in a monograph.
You must come. And if you could give a lecture in French, that
would be even better! I believe one of our books (*La Foi prophétique et le sacré*)[3] was given to you at Eranos last August. I would
be extremely interested to have your impression of it.[4] Don't take
the trouble to respond in detail to this letter. Just tell me, if you
have a free moment, whether you feel the connection between our
theologies. If you share my feeling, I will be delighted. If something remains obscure, let me know about that too.

---

1. [These three essays were published in 1981 as *Le Paradoxe du Monothéisme,* by Éditions de L'Herne in Paris.—Ed.]

2. [L'Université Saint Jean de Jérusalem, Centre international de recher-
che spirituelle comparée, 1974–1988. The organization was succeeded by Les
Cahiers du Groupe d'Etudes Spirituelles Comparées.—Ed.]

3. [*La Foi prophétique et le sacré,* Cahiers de l'Université Saint-Jean-de-
Jérusalem, no. 3 (Paris: Berg International, 1977).—Ed.]

4. [See the review of this book by David L. Miller in *The Journal of the
American Academy of Religion* 46, no. 1 (1978): 94–95.—Ed.]

I await news from you (a good letter in English!). And I wish you good work and good health. I am looking forward to our meeting again at Eranos (though I had to turn down speaking this year since I am swamped with books to finish), and I send you once again, dear colleague and friend, my warm greetings and most sincere affection.

HENRY CORBIN

INTRODUCTION
TO THE SECOND EDITION

It all begins with a fear of *mana*.
    Next there comes the love of tribe.
Native dances, totems, ani-
    Mism and magicians thrive.

Culture grows more complicated.
    Spirits, chiefs in funny hats,
And suchlike spooks are sublimated
    Into gods and ziggurats.

Polyarmed and polyheaded,
    Gods proliferate until
Puristic-minded sages edit
    Their welter into one sweet Will.

This worshipped One grows so enlightened,
    Vast, and high He, in a blur,
Explodes; and men are left as frightened
    Of *mana* as they ever were.

—JOHN UPDIKE[1]

Obsessed, bewildered

By the shipwreck
Of the singular

We have chosen the meaning
Of being numerous.

—GEORGE OPPEN[2]

---

1. John Updike, "Comp. Religion," in *Telephone Poles and Other Poems* (New York: Alfred A. Knopf, 1963), 23.

2. George Oppen, "Of Being Numerous," in *Collected Poems* (New York: New Directions, 1975), 151.

These two contemporary poets, like many others, are alert to a situation felt deeply, even when not known consciously or spoken articulately. I have called it "polytheism." Others use different words.

In a letter following the publication of the first edition of *The New Polytheism*, Henry Corbin, the French scholar of Iranian Sufism, urged discretion with regard to naming this situation about which the poets speak (see Preface). Corbin himself preferred not to call it "polytheism," and in this preference he was following a path already charted by William James at the beginning of this century.

James had been invited to give the Hibbert Lectures at Manchester in 1908. He was sixty-six years old and he had some reticence about traveling to England for the occasion. However, he told a friend that he could not turn down the opportunity to say in popular form something that was important to him. He wanted to argue for something "more" than the merely human and the merely empirical, a "more," which he believed a thoroughgoing and radical empiricism would simply be forced to acknowledge. This "more," as he puts it,

> may be polytheistically or it may be monotheistically conceived of. Fechner [a little-spoken-of philosopher about whom James was extremely enthusiastic]...seems clearly polytheistic; but the word "polytheism" usually gives offense, so perhaps it is better not to use it. Only one thing is certain, and that is the result of our criticism of the absolute: the only way to escape from the paradoxes and perplexities that a consistently thought-out monistic universe suffers from is to be frankly pluralistic...even if the absolute has to have a pluralistic vision...Why should we envelope our many with the "one" that brings so much poison in its train?[3]

_____

3. William James, *A Pluralistic Universe* (Cambridge: Harvard University Press, 1977), 140f.

Although James shies from giving offense by using the word "polytheism," his sentiment is nonetheless hardly weak or unambiguous. Nor was the lectureship of 1908 the first time he had been tempted by the word "polytheism" as a proper designation for the pluralism of his radical philosophical empiricism. In the Gifford Lectures of 1902, subsequently published under the title *The Varieties of Religious Experience*, James noted something about the relation between official theology and popular religion, namely, how they have often been at odds. He said:

> Theism has always shown a tendency to become pantheistic and monistic, and to consider the world a one unit of absolute fact; and this has been at variance with popular or practical theism, which latter has ever been more or less frankly pluralistic, not to say polytheistic, and shown itself perfectly well satisfied with a universe composed of many original principles.[4]

In the "Postscript" to the Gifford lectures, James is even stronger in his language. He says: "All the facts require that the power [i.e., the 'God' of ordinary men] should be both other and larger than our conscious selves...It need not be infinite, it need not be solitary. It might conceivably be only a larger and more godlike self, of which the present self would then be but the mutilated expression, and the universe might conceivably be a collection of such selves,...with no absolute unity realized in it at all. Thus would a sort of polytheism return upon us..." Then James adds, "a polytheism which I do not on this occasion defend, for my only aim at present is to keep the testimony of religious experience clearly within its proper bounds."[5] Again, James is discrete, but surely his testimony is clear.

---

4. William James, *The Varieties of Religious Experience* (New York: Collier Books, 1961), 117.

5. Ibid., 407. In a footnote, James indicates that he already had advanced this notion of a polytheistic psychology in a lecture in 1899.

In 1974, when the first edition of this book was published, I dared to use the word "polytheism" and to defend it. I was following a clue from Nietzsche, rather than from James. Judging by some of the reviews, James was right in thinking that the term would give offense! However, what surprised me more was to discover an uncanny similarity between *The New Polytheism* and books from a wide variety of fields other than religion. I should like to take the opportunity of this second edition to list some of these other works, together with a striking quotation or two from each. My aim is to give a sense of a certain timeliness for the intuition concerning polytheism that Corbin and James, not to mention the poets, have noted, if not named.

The New Polytheism was released in January 1974. Only a few weeks after its appearance, two books came to my attention, both of them translations of French works. One was by the well-known essayist Alain, whose given name was Émile Chartier. He died in 1951, but a portion of his long work, *Les Dieux* (1934), had been translated by Richard Pevear. The second work was a translation by Richard Howard of a book by a contemporary critic, E. M. Cioran. What in France had been titled *Le Mauvais démiurge* was in its American edition called *The New Gods*. First, here are a few sentences from the work by Alain:

> The gods are moments of man...The gods are everywhere. An unknown young man who gives directions, might be Mercury. A wise friend is Mentor, or Minerva. And, as Ulysses is hidden under a beggar's rags, it could just as easily be a god in disguise, is among those that the future will not diminish. The Christian can say no better. Or rather, he ought to say better. Where there is only a man, there is god. Homer already makes this understood when he attributes human passions to the gods, and the petty stratagems of politics as well; to the point that sometimes, as in the case

of the broken truce, the gods seem worse than man...This model is made for us and within our range...The great idea of gods wandering the earth announces a new age, and thoughts less ruled by pride...That is why I think that Chateaubriand went beyond the pagan sublime and even the Christian sublime, in what is perhaps the most beautiful passage in the *Martyrs*. To the Christian who has just given his coat to a beggar, the pagan, in his profound wisdom, says: "No doubt you took him for a god." "No," replies the Christian," I took him for a man.[6]

Cioran's writing carries a similar sense, but the tone is harsher than Alain's and it seems to have more urgency about it, perhaps because it was written thirty-five years later, in 1969. Here is a sample from the 1974 translation:

Polytheism corresponds better to the diversity of our tendencies and our impulses, which it offers the possibility of expressing, of manifesting; each of them being free to tend, according to its nature, toward the god who suits it at the moment. But how deal with a single god? How envisage him, how utilize him? In his presence, we live continually under pressure. Monotheism curbs our sensibility: it deepens us by narrowing us. A system of constraints which affords us an inner dimension at the cost of the flowering of our powers, it constitutes a barrier, it halts our expansion, it throws us out of gear. Surely we were more normal with several gods than we are with only one. If *health* is a criterion, what a setback monotheism turns out to be!...With all due respect to Tertullian, *the soul is naturally pagan*. Any god at all, when he answers to our immediate needs, represents for us an increase of vitality, a stimulus, which is not the case if he is imposed upon us or if he corresponds to no necessity. Paganism's mistake was to have accepted and accumulated too many of them: it died of generosity and excess of understanding—it died from a lack of instinct...There is an underlying polytheism in liberal democracy (call it an

---

6. Alain, *The Gods*, trans. Richard Pevear (New York: New Directions, 1974), 125, 127.

unconscious polytheism); conversely, every authoritarian regime partakes of a disguised monotheism. Curious, the effects of a monotheistic logic: a pagan, once he became a Christian, tended toward intolerance. Better to founder with a horde of accommodating gods than to prosper in a despot's shadow! In an age when, lacking religious conflicts, we witness ideological ones, the question raised for us is indeed the one which haunted a waning antiquity: how to renounce so many gods for just one?[7]

These lines with their haunting questions, along with those of Alain, were already prefigured in some striking sentences written by an American poet, William Carlos Williams, in 1920:

Giants in the dirt. The gods, the Greek gods, smothered in filth and ignorance. The race is scattered over the world. Where is its home? Find it if you've the genius. Here Hebe with a sick jaw and cruel husband—her mother left no place for a brain to grow. Herakles rowing boats on Berry's Creek! Zeus is a country doctor without a taste for coin jingling. Supper is of a bastard nectar on rare nights for they will come—the rare nights! The ground lifts and out sally the heroes of Sophocles, of Æschylus. They go seeping down into our hearts, they rain upon us and in the bog they sink again down through the white roots, down—to a saloon back of the railroad switch where they have that girl, you know, the one that should have been Venus by the lust that's in her. They've got her down there among the railroad men. A Crusade couldn't rescue her. Up to jail—or call it down to Limbo—the Chief of Police our Pluto. It's all of the gods, there's nothing else worth writing of. They are the same men they always were—but fallen. Do they dance now, they that danced beside Helicon? They dance much as they did then, only, few have an eye for it, through the dirt and fumes.[8]

---

7. E.M. Cioran, *The New Gods,* trans. Richard Howard (New York: The New York Times Books, 1974), 22, 24, 26.

8. William Carlos Williams, *Kora in Hell: Improvisations* (San Francisco: City Lights Books, 1974), 50f.

One of the few who has had an eye for it is psychologist James Hillman. An essay of his from 1971 is reviewed in Chapter Four, and that essay, in a revised and expanded form, is included as an Appendix to this new edition. Hillman's work is written out of a Jungian background, whereas another who had "had an eye" for a polytheistic perspective, namely, Norman O. Brown, writes from a Freudian base.

Brown's sensibility in the direction of the gods was expressed implicitly in his book on Freud in 1959 (*Life Against Death*) and explicitly in the year just prior to the first edition of *The New Polytheism*. In a book entitled *Closing Time,* Brown drew prominently on words that the poet H.D. (Hilda Doolittle) had written in a note to Freud on the occasion of his coming to live in England. The phrase was simple: "To greet the return of the gods!" Brown placed these words in the context of "waiting for the return of the theocratic age" in our time.[9]

In the following year (1974), Brown linked his earlier study of Freud to myths of Greek gods and goddesses in a series of tapes released under the title of H.D.'s phrase. *To Greet the Return of the Gods* included oral essays (for is not story telling a mode proper to mythology?) on Actaeon, Dionysos, *The Georgics,* Aristophanes's *The Birds,* the Muses (four long tapes!), Daphne, the Creation of the World of the Alphabet, and so on. Here is a sample:

> Love like a shadow flies when substance love pursues; pursuing that that flies, and flying what pursues. The stricken hart, emblem of love incurable. The god of love, or Dionysos, the great hunter, is Apollo chasing Daphne. To free us from our servitude: it is we who are the stag; the soul haunted by the hound of heaven ...

9. Norman O. Brown, *Closing Time* (New York: Random House, 1973), 41.

> Very few are the Actaeons to whom destiny gives the power
> to contemplate Diana naked, and the power to become so
> enamored of the beautiful harmony of the body of nature
> that they are transformed into deer; inasmuch as they are
> no longer the hunters but the hunted. Therefore, from the
> vulgar, civil and ordinary man he was, he becomes as free
> as a deer, and an inhabitant of the wilderness; he lives
> like a god.[10]

I did not know about Brown's tapes while working on the
final revision of this book's manuscript. Nor had I seen the publication (in the same year, 1973) of a work directly linked to the
theme of polytheism by a Heideggerian philosopher, Vincent
Vycinas. This thinker's works, *Search of Gods* (1972) and *Our
Cultural Agony* (1973), deepen the psychological polytheism of
Hillman and Brown in the direction of a radical ontology. For
example, Vycinas wrote:

> Things are founded in the gods. Even during the phases of
> cultural upheavals, mix-ups, conquests, or times when cul-
> ture loses its strength and its holding power in man's living
> situations, it is still the gods, often concealed and unborn
> gods, who are the cultural dominating principles wherein
> things are founded. Man's task is to search for them. Even
> during the "Twilight of the Gods," gods—concealed or with-
> drawn—carry the meanings and the realness of things.[11]

> In our god less contemporary world, a creative and for-
> ward-looking man must, first of all, discover his own self,

---

10. The tapes were recorded and distributed by the Office of Instruc-
tional Services of the University of California at Santa Cruz. This excerpt
may be found in Norman O. Brown, "Metamorphoses II: Actaeon," *The American Poetry Review* 1, no. 1 (Nov.–Dec. 1972): 40, where it was published in
advance of the release of the tapes.

11. Vincent Vycinas, *Search of Gods* (The Hague: Martinus Nijhoff, 1972),
79. Cf. also his earlier work *Earth and Gods* (The Hague: Martinus Nijhoff,
1961).

lost on the pathless terrain whereon he is set or whereon he is thrown by the powers of destiny...Doing this, he is bound to free his inner self toward the gods.[12]

Philosophy begins in the twilight of gods, where man becomes an outcast from the dance of the gods, and because of this he, already with his very first steps, is directed into the process of his struggle, pressing his way back into the works of the gods—he is on the way of a search for new gods. The process of philosophy is, historically, the process of its deviation from mythical thought. During the process philosophy seems to acquire its own stand on its own grounds. Only gradually during its historical development, does philosophy begin to realize that these grounds owe themselves to the abysmal or chaotic ground of pre-philosophical or mythical thought. By seeing itself as merely a province of mythical thought, philosophy overcomes itself; it does so by heading towards the dawn of new gods.[13]

William Shepherd carried forward Brown's work in 1976,[14] just as James Ogilvy continued in 1977 the philosophical work of Vycinas, though this latter made no explicit reference to Vycinas.[15] Whereas Shepherd preferred the word "polysymbolic," Ogilvy uses the term " polytheism" and argues for an alternative to a "monotheistic hermeneutic" in a "pluralism of parapolitics." Ogilvy has a section of his book specifically on the Greek gods, and in this way his work is not unlike that of Naomi Goldenberg.

---

12. Vincent Vycinas, *Our Cultural Agony* (The Hague: Martinus Nijhoff, 1973), 193.

13. Ibid., 29.

14. William C. Shepherd, *Symbolical Consciousness: A Commentary on Love's Body* (Missoula, Mont.: Scholars Press, 1976).

15. James A. Ogilvy, *Many-Dimensional Man: Decentralizing Self, Society, and the Sacred* (New York: Oxford University Press, 1977). Ogilvy's book "combines a theory of the decentralized self with a theory of decentralized society in order to seek within the self those paradigms of interpretation necessary to sustain pluralism." (p. 322)

In *Changing the Gods* (1979), she linked the theological, philosophical, psychological, and political themes of these other
works to the women's movement.[16]

There have been other witnesses to the intuition concerning
polytheism since this book was first published[17]—in psychology
and sociology, in philosophy and theology, in political theory and
aesthetics—but perhaps these few instances will begin to give a
sense that there may well have been something to the saying of
the German poet Rainer Maria Rilke, when he wrote:

> This heart...belongs to the gods
> unendingly.[18]

Eternally and immortally, the gods seem to be the faces of
what we must face, multifaceted resources of meaning, heart-
felt, deep-down.[19] It is no wonder, then, that Rilke asks:

> Shall we reject our age-old friendship, the great
> never-soliciting gods, because the hard
> steel we have strictly schooled does not know them
> or shall we suddenly seek them on a map?[20]

If this book has not managed to be a "map," at least it was the
beginning of a "seeking." Perhaps on the occasion of this second
edition, two modifications may be permitted, one having to do

---

16. Naomi Goldenberg, *Changing the Gods* (Boston: Beacon Press, 1979).

17. There were also arguments in this direction prior to 1974. See Robert
A. Dahl, *Polyarchy: Participation and Opposition* (New Haven: Yale University
Press, 1971); William E. Connolly, *The Bias of Pluralism* (New York: Atherton
Press, 1969); and Henry Alonzo Myers, *Systematic Pluralism: A Study in Meta-
physics* (Ithaca: Cornell University Press, 1961).

18. Rainer Maria Rilke, *Sonnets to Orpheus,* trans. M.D. Herter Norton
(New York: Norton and Co., 1962), 23.

19. For a more concrete work in this direction, see *Facing the Gods,* ed.
James Hillman (Irving, Texas: Spring Publications, 1980).

20. Rilke, *Sonnets,* 63.

with *behavior and consciousness,* the other having to do with *story and image.*

(1) *Ethos and mythos.* Especially in Chapter Five, but also implicit here and there throughout the book, there seems to be a suggestion that we behave (*ethos*) the patterns (*mythos*) of the stories of gods and goddesses. For example, one finds the following sentence: "The military-industrial complex is Hera-Heracles-Hephaestus." Or again: "Activism...is the work of Heracles." This is misleading, I now sense.

The idea is not that myths describe or prescribe actions. They do not symbolize univocal behaviors. Rather, they express articulately in ways that we often are not able, our feelings or thoughts, our consciousness or sense, concerning any behavior. Oedipus, for example, is not some particular moral or ethical activity, say, between the persons of Father, Mother, and Son. Oedipus is not something sociological at all, or at least not in the first instance. He is more psychological. Perhaps one could think of Oedipus as the epiphany that comes to pass when one-anyone at all—a Father or a Mother or a Child—either Son or Daughter—interprets or feels, wittingly or unwittingly, a sense of self or relationship in terms of an intimate, family-like triangle in which love and hate figure prominently at the same time.

The same would be true for other complexes, other figurings of the gods. Polytheistic perspective, I should like to imagine, makes mythos of ethos, not morality out of ancient myth. Each myth has many behavioral manifestations, and every behavior is susceptible of being felt and known in plural perspectives. We do not behave the gods; rather, their behaviors are our senses, our meanings.

(2) *Story and image.* There is a similar danger, I now believe, in the enthusiasm for story and for narrative form that is spelled out especially in Chapters Two and Three. One finds, for example, sentences like the following:

> Thinking monotheistically about the deepest matters of the heart and spirit cannot put man in touch with life as can another sort of *theologia*: the telling of the tales of the gods and goddesses in personified concreteness.

Or again:

> Narrative theology may be the only way in our time to reviv-ify an irrelevant doctrinal theology that has abstracted itself out of life by managing to kill God.

Sentiments like these may need some qualification.

It is not that anything is "wrong" with narrative expression. Nor do I wish to take back anything I have said recommending attention to it, either in this book or in my earlier work, *Gods and Games*.[21] The danger I see lies rather in how one views a story or how a story is used. Narrative form is no better than abstract ideation if it is used ideologically, that is, for ego security. This is particularly important to note in a time when story form enjoys a more than passing popularity in philosophy, theology, and liter-ary criticism.[22]

Patricia Berry and Ted Estess have each written what I take to be extremely important articles in which they register the

---

21. David L. Miller, *Gods and Games: Toward a Theology of Play* (New York: Harper and Row, 1973), 164–69.

22. See, for example, Stephen Crites, "The Narrative Quality of Expe-rience," *Journal of the American Academy of Religion* 39, no. 3 (Sept. 1971): 297ff.; Sam Keen, *To a Dancing God: Notes of a Spiritual Traveler* (New York: Harper and Row, 1970); Religion as Story, ed. James B. Wiggins (New York: Harper and Row, 1975); Michael Novak, *Ascent of the Mountain, Flight of the Dove: An Invitation to Religious Studies* (New York: Harper and Row, 1971); John Dunne, *A Search for God in Time and Memory* (New York: Macmillan, 1970); James W. McClendon Jr., *Biography as Theology: How Life Stories Can Remake Today's Theology* (Nashville: Abingdon, 1974); Harvey Cox, *The Feast of Fools: A Theological Essay on Festivity and Fantasy* (Cambridge University Press, 1969); Robert Scholes and Robert Kellogg, *The Nature of Narrative* (New York: Oxford University Press, 1966).

reticence that now compels me. Estess was writing from a religious and literary perspective. His argument, grounded in the writings of Samuel Beckett, but surely not limited to Beckett, took note of something that every person senses: namely, that from time to time life may come to be experienced as "an inenarrable contraption." In such an event, precisely when our various stories fail us, whether individually or collectively, story-form is of no more use to ego than is theoretical explanation. To this point, Estess quotes Beckett, first from *The Unnameable* and then from *Stories and Texts for Nothing*:

> ...his story is the story to be told, but he has no story, he hasn't been in story, it's not certain, he's in his own story, unimaginable, unspeakable...

> No need of a story, a story is not compulsory, just a life, that's the mistake I made, one of the mistakes, to have wanted a story for myself, whereas life alone is enough.

Estess indicates that similar examples could be cited from John Barth, Donald Barthelme, and other contemporary writers.[23]

The point, I take it, is that if stories are used to shore up ego against its ruin, a ruin consisting precisely in failed autobiographical, familial, marital, educational, religious, political, national, social, and cosmic stories; that is, if stories are believed to be a crutch that will help ego hobble back into a modicum of control, "master of fate" and "captain of soul"—then the stories of the gods may be as disappointing as the social ideologies and the monotheistic theologies that replaced them. Enthusiasm for narrative form can become just one more idolatry.

Patricia Berry is a Jungian analyst, and her concern about narrative, though not unlike Estess's, comes more out of ex-

---

23. Ted L. Estess, "The Inenarrable Contraption: Reflections on the Metaphor of Story," *Journal of the American Academy of Religion* 42, no. 3 (Sept. 1974): 415–34.

periences of brokenness in life. In analysis, again and again, there is a temptation, just at the point of intrusion of difficult experience, strong emotion, or stunning insight, to couch the matter perhaps a little too quickly in the context of a story. One's ego can handle things a little better if it knows the plot: where it came from in the past; what its relation is to other characters in the psyche; how it may develop; where the denouement is; and what the ending or outcome may be. Story comes into the therapeutic session often as a defense mechanism, a way of defending against depth and deepening, a way of taking conscious control of the radical experience that humbles one.

Berry is particularly concerned with our dreams and what we do with them. She writes:

> This brings us to the…most important difficulty of narrative: it tends to become ego's trip. The hero has a way of finding himself in the midst of any story. He can turn anything into a parable of a way to make it and stay on top. The continuity in a story becomes *his* ongoing heroic movement. Hence when we read a dream as narrative there is nothing more ego-natural than to take the sequence of movement as a progression culminating in the dreamer's just reward or defeat. The way a story encapsulates one into it as protagonist corrupts the dream into a mirror in which ego sees only its concerns.[24]

If one function of a dream is precisely to break ego's narrative (think of Jacob and his Ladder, or the Shepherds at the first Christmas), then to place a dream's image in the *personal* story is to lose an important opportunity, even if the opportunity involves risk and discomfort.[25]

---

24. Patricia Berry, "An Approach to the Dream," in *Echo's Subtle Body: Contributions to an Archetypal Psychology* (Thompson, Conn.: Spring Publications, 2017), 67.

25. I have made a similar point in an article that contrasts two perspec-

In *The New Polytheism,* I had originally intended story forms, the myths of the gods and goddesses, to be seen as breaking the monopoly of abstract theological explanations, very much as a striking image (a mood, a personal mess, an Angel) smashes the narrative continuity of a personal life story. That is, stories were not to be viewed as images of gods and goddesses that secured ego's various accounts of how things are, "getting it together" for my life. Rather, stories were to be viewed imaginally (as Corbin has properly insisted in the Preface). Like Angels and dreams and ego pathologies, stories are images, or so I had supposed and now explicitly propose.

Thus, though the polytheistic theology of this book is grounded in stories of the gods and goddesses, the work is not written from the perspective of narrative theology. Rather, the perspective here is that which I have come to call *theologia imaginalis,* "imaginal theologizing," a perspective for which Gaston Bachelard, as well as Henry Corbin, has laid solid philosophical foundation.[26]

Bachelard, like Estess and Berry, has shown how story, if it is not viewed imaginally, can seduce one away from depths of experience and plenitudes of meaning, which the story itself carries. Bachelard writes: "The art of the story teller is so great, the

---

tives on narrative: fairy-tale perspective and mythic perspective: "Fairy Tale or Myth?," *Spring: An Annual of Archetypal Psychology and Jungian Thought* (1976): 157–64.

26. I have developed the notion of a *theologia imaginalis* in more detail in "Theologia Imaginalis," in *The Archaeology of the Imagination: Deconstruction and Hermeneutics,* ed. Charles E. Winquist (Chico, Calif.: Scholars Press, 1981); "Theology's Ego/Religion's Soul," *Spring: An Annual of Archetypal Psychology and Jungian Thought* (1980); and "Introduction: The Idea of a Polytheistic, Archetypal Theology," in David L. Miller, *Christs: Meditations on Archetypal Images in Christian Theology* (New Orleans: Spring Journal Books, 2005).

rationalizations evoked so comfortable, that one could under-estimate the imaginal weight of images."[27] The image breaks the horizontal narrative movement. Bachelard agrees with the philosopher Schelling: "Only the vertical direction [i.e., height and depth] provides an active spiritual meaning.[28] "Verticality [is a] pause in narrative during which the reader is invited to dream."[29] (Again, Jacob and the Shepherds!) Thus, the most fundamental imaginal meaning, that is, the full pleroma of polytheistic richness, is "not experienced from day to day on the thread of a narrative or in the telling of a story."[30] Bachelard is firm in this point, and it seems to me that his philosophy of the imagination matches the cultural situation described by Estess and the experience of psyche told by Berry.

Nonetheless, Bachelard acknowledges that it is *perspective* that is at issue here, rather than an either/or choosing between actual stories and actual images. He shows that a mythic story, if lived thoroughly, not as an explanation for ego, but as vertical image, may indeed function as an *image-conteuse*[31] or as

---

27. Gaston Bachelard, *La Terre et les rêveries de la volonté* (Paris: Librairie José Corti, 1948), 254.

28. Ibid., 364.

29. Gaston Bachelard, *The Poetics of Space*, trans. Maria Jolas (New York: Orion Press, 1964), 162.

30. Ibid., 5. Compare these other statements by Bachelard in *The Poetics of Reverie: Childhood, Language, and the Cosmos*, trans. Daniel Russell (New York: Orion Press, 1969): "I do not know how to dream on a novel while following the entire story line. In such narratives, I find such an enormity of becoming that I rest myself by stopping off at a psychological site where I can make a passage mine by dreaming it" (p. 75); and "In dreaming on the family of the gods, we would slip into biographies, but the mythologem of childhood invites us to greater dreams" (p. 133).

31. Gaston Bachelard, *La Terre et les rêveries du repos* (Paris: Librairie José Corti, 1948), 163.

a *légende-image*.[32] In the first of these instances, one comes to notice that a certain image tends in the direction of plot. The image gives thickness or density, thickening the plot of life, leading to make-believe, to imagination, the domain of *mundus imaginalis*. In the second, the experience is that of a story not being sensed as linear development, not with a before and after, neither coming from some "where" nor going to another "where." Rather, the sense is synchronistic and holistic: the story has the immediacy of a total complex, all at once, here and now, a *légende-image*.

This is just the sense that I am after in *The New Polytheism*. It is therefore why I am especially grateful for the letter sent by Henry Corbin, now a Preface to this edition, in which he interpreted the polytheistic perspective of this work in terms of his own *mundus imaginalis*. I happily echo his words: "Agreed, agreed!"

I am grateful, too, to Spring Publications for making possible a second edition of this book. Particularly am I indebted to James Hillman for being willing to include as an Appendix his essay, which was so important to this work's genesis. Indeed, that essay makes me realize that the words of George Oppen, "We have chosen the meaning/Of being numerous," are true only because: the meaning of being numerous has chosen us.

---

32. Ibid., 163.

ONE

AN EXPLODED CULTURAL SPHERE:
THE DEATH OF GOD AND THE REBIRTH OF THE GODS

For the individual to set up his own ideal and derive from
it his laws, his pleasures, and his rights—*that* has perhaps
been hitherto regarded as the most monstrous of all human
aberrations, and as idolatry in itself; in fact, the few who
have ventured to do this have always needed to apolo-
gize...It was in the marvelous art and capacity for creating
Gods—in polytheism—that this impulse was permitted to
discharge it self, it was here that it became purified, per-
fected, and ennobled...Monotheism, on the contrary, the
rigid consequence of the doctrine of one normal human
being—consequently the belief in a normal God, beside
whom there are only false, spurious Gods—has perhaps
been the greatest danger of mankind in the past...In polytheism man's free-thinking and many-sided thinking has
a prototype set up: the power to create for himself new and
individual eyes, always newer and more individualized.[1]

There is a bright, new future lurking in these lines, still
waiting to be understood. Friedrich Nietzsche, the prophetic philosopher and madman of the last century, once
again becomes our mouthpiece. Formerly he supplied our culture with its words of felt desperation: the death of God, nihil-
ism, decadence, eternal recurrence, and the will to power. These
were articulations for a time when man was caught in between—
between two world wars, between religion and science, between
Russian communism and the Western Christian world, between

---

1. Friedrich Nietzsche, "The Greatest Utility of Polytheism," in *Joyful Wisdom*, trans. Thomas Commons (New York: Ungar, 1960), 178–80.

cold war apathy and hot guerrilla confrontations in a third world, between Oriental wisdom and Judeo-Christian history, between an ever dichotomous, alienated, schizophrenic existence of proliferating polarities. This "betweenness" is a time of the double lack and the double not: the time of "the No-more of the gods that have fled and the Not-yet of the god that is coming."[2] Nietzsche had helped us to see in advance that entrapment in this "between" would mean a relativism and a transvaluation of all moral values, whose proper name he also told us would shock the world when it was announced straightforwardly: the death of God!

But this is all old hat. In the meantime we have managed to go on, and in the going on we have been compelled by new themes: *Future Shock*; the rediscovery of the sacred in odd places, even in Jesus for some; Consciousness III and the *Greening of America*; a *Love Story* by Segal and a *Seagull* by Bach; a new batch of science fiction; ritual happenings in drama where the theater of the absurd used to reign; a flowery counterculture; new sensuality concerning nature and new sexuality concerning the body; veritable expansions of consciousness everywhere.

Perhaps nothing is more remarkable about the way we have been going on than the diversity of our new themes and their accompanying lifestyles. When one searches for a least common denominator in our present sensibilities—a new root metaphor, some emerging center of concern—what one discovers is that the factors of our meaning simply dance all over the map of our being. In order to name our present condition interpreters have had to rely on a strange set of words.

In tracing our psychology, Charles Baudouin speaks of *polymorphic* meaning and being. In speaking of the nature of thinking

---

2. Martin Heidegger, *Existence and Being* (Chicago: Henry Regnery Co., 1949), 289.

required for contemporary understanding, Philip Wheelwright points to *plurisignificative* knowing and communicating. Norman O. Brown talks about polymorphous reality as a key to our history, and Ray Hart names the deepest aspect of our literate articulations of reality with the phrase *polysemous* functioning of imaginal discourse. If we try to make sense of our society Michael Novak suggests it will help to think of America as a *pluralistic* community of radically unmeltable ethnics. Concerning government and political science, Robert Dahl speaks of *polyarchy*.

Nietzsche's name for all this is polytheism. He says it straight out rather than hiding the radicalness of where we are behind a barrage of academic verbiage. By polytheism Nietzsche means that lurking in all the "poly" and plural abstractions of our scholarship is something very concrete and real. We have suffered a death of God. But we discover a new opportunity after the passing of the first shadow of despair that comes from the loss of a single center holding all things together.

The death of God was, in fact, the demise of a monotheistic way of thinking and speaking about God and a monotheistic way of thinking and speaking about human meaning and being generally. The announcement of the death of God was the obituary of a useless single-minded and one-dimensional norm of a civilization that has been predominantly monotheistic, not only in its religion, but also in its politics, its history, its social order, its ethics, and its psychology. When released from the tyrannical imperialism of monotheism by the death of God, man has the opportunity of discovering new dimensions hidden in the depths of reality's history. He may discover a new freedom to acknowledge variousness and many-sidedness. He may find, as if for the first time, a new potency to create imaginatively his hopes and desires, his laws and pleasures.

The point Nietzsche is making is that our personal and social bondage has been a slavery to a specific kind of *theological* thinking and speaking, and therefore our new sensibility is also a theological breakthrough at base. Nietzsche can be concrete where other analysts of culture are abstract; he can be materially realistic where others are formally intellectualistic. The death of God gives rise to the rebirth of the gods. We are polytheists.

Polytheism is the name given to a specific religious situation. The situation is characterized by plurality, a plurality that manifests itself in many forms. Socially, polytheism is a situation in which there are various values, patterns of social organization, and principles by which man governs his political life. These values, patterns, and principles sometimes mesh harmoniously, but more often they war with one another to be elevated as the single center of normal social order. Such a situation would be sheer anarchy and chaos were it not possible to identify the many orders as each containing a coherence of its own. Socially understood, polytheism is eternally in unresolvable conflict with social monotheism, which in its worst form is fascism and in its less destructive forms is imperialism, capitalism, feudalism and monarchy. There is an incipient polytheism always lurking in democracy. This polytheism will surface during the history of democracies if the civilization does not first succumb to anarchy. In calling our time polytheist, we are saying something about the state of democracy in our time.

Polytheism is not only a social reality; it is also a philosophical condition. It is that reality experienced by men and women when Truth with a capital "T" cannot be articulated reflectively according to a single grammar, a single logic, or a single symbol-system. It is a situation that exists when metaphors, stories, anecdotes, aphorisms, puns, dramas, and movies, with all their mysterious ambiguity, seem more compelling than the rhetoric of political, religious, and philosophical systems. They seem more compelling than tightly argued and logically coherent explanations of self and society because they allow for multiple meanings to exist simultaneously, as if Truth, Goodness, and Beauty can never be contained in a logic that allows for only one of the following: good versus evil, light versus dark, truth versus fiction, reality versus illusion, being versus becoming. In a philosophically polytheistic situation the "new science" of the time will break forth with principles of relativism, indeterminacy, plural logic systems, irrational numbers; substances that do not have substance, such as quarks; double explanations for light; and black holes in the middle of actual realities.

Psychologically, polytheism is a matter of the radical experience of equally real, but mutually exclusive aspects of the self. Personal identity cannot seem to be fixed. Normalcy cannot be defined. The person experiences himself as many selves each of which is felt to have autonomous power, a life of its own, coming and going on its own and without regard to the centered will of a single ego. Yet surprisingly this experience is not sensed as a pathology. One gets along quite well in reality; in fact, the very disparateness of the multifaceted self seems to have survival power. It seems to carry with it a certain advantage in the face of the times. If the academic psychology by which the self explains the self to itself is monotheistic and cannot provide sufficient rationale for understanding in such a time, then the psychology will itself have to be reformed polytheistically.

The word polytheism is used for these social, philosophical, and psychological manifestations of plurality in everyday life because behind them is a *religious* situation. Religiously, polytheism is the worship of many gods and goddesses. Though monotheism with its exclusive forms—say, in Christianity,

Judaism, and Islam—rules out the possibility of polytheism in religion, polytheism, in a curious way, includes a monotheism of sorts. The great polytheist cultures—Greek, Hindu, Egyptian, Mesopotamian, American Indian—have in actual practice been composed of communities of men and women who worship one god or goddess, or at least they worship one at a time—Athena, Vishnu, Ra, Baal, Wakan Tanka. The *theologies* of these peoples, however, affirm the reality and the worship of many. This implies that a polytheistic religion is actually a polytheistic theology, a system of symbolizing reality in a plural way in order to account for all experience, but that the religious practice is composed of consecutive monotheisms. Similarly, it would seem possible that one might profess a monotheistic faith, but need a poly-theistic theology to account for all of one's experiences in the life-context of that faith. Thus, we need to distinguish between polytheism and monotheism in religion on the one hand and in theology on the other. The former has to do with a practice, a behavior, and the latter has to do with the explanation sys-tem needed to account for one's experiences in that practice and behavior. The social, philosophical, and psychological polythe-ism of our time is an experience that is sufficiently radical to call for a *polytheistic* theology.

This implies that our experience of social, intellectual, and psychological worlds is religious—that is, it is so profound and far-reaching that only a theological explanation can account for it fully. But what does this mean about the theological expla-nations, about the nature of the gods and goddesses? It means that the gods and goddesses are the names of powers, or forces, which have autonomy and are not conditioned by or affected by social and historical events, by human will or reason, or by per-sonal and individual factors. This is one meaning of our use of the word "Immortal" as it is applied to divinities. The gods are not contingent upon the conditions of mortality. Insofar as they manifest themselves in life they are felt to be informing powers that give shape to social, intellectual, and personal behavior. The gods and goddesses are the names of the plural patterns of our existence. Their stories are the paradigms and symbols that allow us to account for, to express, and to celebrate those multiple aspects of our reality that otherwise would seem fragmented and anarchic.

In Western culture, the polytheistic theology that would enable us to "name" our plurality, so as to obtain an Archimedean point of leverage on life, died with the collapse of the Greek culture. From then on our explanation systems, whether theological, sociological, political, historical, philosophical, or psychological, have in the main been monotheistic. That is, they have been operating according to fixed concepts and categories that were controlled by a logic that demanded a rigorous and decisive either/or: either true or false, either this or that, either beautiful or ugly, either good or evil. It is this monotheistic thinking that fails a people in a time when experience becomes self-consciously pluralistic, radically both/and. Monotheistic thinking is especially ill-equipped to handle pluralistic understanding when the multiple meanings flowing through social and psychological reality seem to have autonomous power, like the gods and goddesses, and when the multifaceted layers of reality, like the divinities, seem not to be in control of the society or the individual at the very time when that society and that individual feel freed into the openness of new possibility, shocked into a radically liberating future.

There have, of course, been remnants of polytheistic religious thinking hiding here and there in Western modes of understanding. The stories of the gods and goddesses have had staying power in the underground or countercultural tradition of the West. Their symbol-systems are to be found in Roman polytheism, in gnosticism, in alchemy, in kabbalism and in other forms of mysticism, in Neoplatonism (for example, in the eighteenth-century Englishman Thomas Taylor), in the people's tradition of folk and fairy tales, and sometimes in drama, novel, and poetry (for example, William Blake). But these movements were either not taken seriously enough, were thought to be ornamental and frivolous as explanation-systems of human life, or were systematically suppressed by the Church or the scientific interests of the university. Thus polytheistic symbol-systems are not now available to a society or a self that is rediscovering its radical plurality.

The tension that has existed in the West between monotheism and polytheism can be seen in the curious case of a symbol which has meant a great deal to man throughout Occidental history. This is that of the circle, a symbol especially useful in seeing the point about polytheism, the point of the rebirth of the gods in the wake of the death of God as understood by monotheistic theology.[3]

Six centuries before Christ, Xenophanes of Colophon was tired of all the stories by all the poets about all the gods and goddesses. His new story was one of "getting it all together," and his abstract name for its presiding "deity" was the *sphere,* a single God as he would have had it. Perhaps he had Plato's point in mind: that the sphere is the most perfect figure because all points on its surface are equidistant from the center. Whatever his reasoning, Xenophanes identified the circular shape of the sphere with monotheism.

---

3. The account that follows is taken from an essay by Jorge Luis Borges, "Pascal's Sphere," in *Other Inquisitions, 1937–1952* (New York: Washington Square Press, 1966), 5–8.

Some years later, Parmenides of Elea used the same image for a different purpose. He called "being" (that monotheistic deity of philosophical reasoning) a well-rounded sphere whose force is constant from the center in any direction. This view was shared by Empedocles of Agrigentum, but the reference shifted from the abstract word "being" to the equally abstract "cosmos," which Empedocles thought of as an endless *sphairos* that rejoices in its circular solitude. These Greek philosophers provided a figural representation of human meaning that Christian monotheistic theologians would later find congenial. All is organized around a single center; the horizon is fixed and secure. So Dante, preserving not only Ptolemaic astronomy but also Christian theology, imagined the earth as an immovable sphere at the center of the universe, around which nine concentric spheres revolve. The first seven are the planetary heavens (Moon, Mercury, Venus, Sun, Mars, Saturn, and Jupiter). The eighth is the Heaven of Fixed Stars, and the ninth is the Crystalline Heaven, the *Primum Mobile*, surrounded by the Empyrean of pure light.

But the circle exploded sometime between Dante's then and Nietzsche's now. William Butler Yeats wrote,

> Turning and turning in the widening gyre The falcon cannot hear the falconer; Things fall apart; the centre cannot hold; Mere anarchy is loosed upon the world.[4]

What Copernicus did to the Ptolemaic view of the natural world—exploding the horizons of an infinitely expanding universe whose center is suddenly unknown—happened also in the social sphere with a relativizing of all truth and morality.

---

4. Reprinted, with permission of Macmillan Publishing Co., Inc., from "The Second Coming," *Collected Poems of W. B. Yeats.* Copyright 1924 by Macmillan Publishing Co., Inc., renewed 1952 by Bertha Georgia Yeats. Permission also by A. P. Watt & Son, Ltd.

Contemporary life often feels anarchistic: no horizons, fences, boundaries, and no center to prove one securely close to home.

But certainly the exploded circle is a potential source of a very different set of feelings: liberation, openness, release from fixation and from the oppression of centers and boundaries of all sorts. What is needed to feel the exploded circle in a constructive way is a different sort of seeing, a seeing different from the enclosing, circular sort of Parmenides, Empedocles, Xenophanes, and Dante. And such a way has been preparing itself all along.

In a book called the Asclepius, one part of a larger set of works referred to by the title *Corpus Hermeticum,* we find a different imaging of the circle by one Hermes Trismegistus (Hermes Thrice-Greatest). He defined God as "an intelligible sphere whose center is everywhere and whose circumference is nowhere." The thirteenth-century *Roman de la Rose* attributes this same definition to Plato. It is repeated in the sixteenth-century *Pantagruel,* and Giordano Bruno applied the definition to Copernicus's universe, saying, "We can state with certainty that the universe is all center, or that the center of the universe is everywhere and the circumference is nowhere" (*De la causa, principio e uno,* V). Nicholas of Cusa, a Catholic bishop in western Germany a century before Bruno and the Pantagruel, was a proponent of the same definition of God. And Carl Jung, the Swiss psychologist, used the same phrase in his own way.

> So far, I have found no stable or definite center in the unconscious and I don't believe such a center exists. I believe that the thing which I call the Self is an ideal center, equidistant between the Ego and the Unconscious...As nature aspires to express itself, so does man, and the Self is that dream of totality...The Self is a circle whose center is everywhere and whose circumference is nowhere.[5]

---

5. From a conversation cited in Miguel Serrano, *C. G. Jung and Hermann*

When Pascal uses this term of many referents (God, society, self, universe), he makes it apply to nature, saying in the *Pensées,* "It [nature] is an infinite sphere, the center of which is everywhere, the circumference nowhere." It may be noted that Pascal first wrote "frightful [*effroyable*] sphere."[6]

The experience of the loss of a center is indeed *frightful* at first, whether sensed by a culture or by an individual person. But after the fright passes, one notices a new sense of liberty: how everywhere one stands is a center, a new center, and the universe of meaning is not limited to a tight little horizon, a vicious circle of a single mind and lifetime. Today, we have a real sense of the hermetic meaning of the horizonless circle without boundaries and limits. We have only yet to notice that this experience applies to God and society, self and universe, in such a way as to imply that when the center is everywhere it is, in fact, multiple. Everywhere a person stands is a social and a psychological center. And multiple means polytheism.

Polytheism is not a historical or an academic matter. It is a feeling for the deep, abiding, urgent, and exciting tension that arises when, with a radical experience of the plurality of both social and psychological life, one discovers that a single story, a monovalent logic, a rigid theology, and a confining morality are not adequate to help in understanding the nature of real meaning. Such a situation is not a matter simply for theologians or philosophers; it is a basic tension at the heart of the experience of all men and women. The tension has likely existed in all times, but it has surfaced radically in our age and calls now for a recollection, a new look. at what polytheism was really all about.

Hesse: A Record of Two Friendships, trans. Frank MacShane (New York: Schocken Books, 1968), 50, 56.

6. Borges, "Pascal's Sphere," 8.

It may be that this need to recall an old symbol-system for new purposes may be behind the recent interest in the occult, in magic, in extraterrestrial life, in Hindu India and Buddhist Japan, in multidemoned China, in sorcery, in new forms of multiple family life, in communes, in the "new religions," and many other alternative lifestyles and meaning-systems that have been hitherto foreign. This recent burgeoning of multiple modes of meaning could have the effect of leading us unrealistically into symbol-systems that are not effective in Western consciousness and behavior. But they may have another effect too. They may alert us to the rediscovery of the sources of multiplicity in our own tradition. The gods and goddesses of *Greece* are our heritage. Sooner or later it is they who will reappear, if only as stories that account for the interaction of Western culture with that foreignness which the Greeks insisted on calling "barbarian." This is not to say that the invasion of our cultural consciousness by polytheistic systems from Hindu Asia, Buddhist and Shinto Japan, primitive Africa and the Americas, is not a part of the new cultural polytheism. It is, to be sure. But only modes of meaning indigenous to our own ways of thinking and feeling will suffice to help us *understand* the new polytheism of which much beyond Greece will be a part.

In order to understand the relation of the Greek Immortals to the new polytheism it will be important for us to do several things.

1. We will need to explore the theological and philosophical relationship between monotheism and polytheism in order to determine whether these are mutually exclusive modes of consciousness. Such an exploration will inquire into the differences, if any, between social plurality and deep religious polytheism. We will attempt an understanding of these issues in Chapter Two by way of seeing what is really at stake in a recent debate on monotheism and polytheism that appears in two books, one by a

theologian and social interpreter and the other by a philosopher and culture-historian.

2. Having explored the exclusiveness or inclusiveness of monotheism and polytheism, we will be able, also in Chapter Two, to probe the *theology* of ancient polytheistic religion. This will help us to answer the question of the resourcefulness of poly-theistic theology in providing our modern pluralistic situation with a way to articulate our diversity. The answer will hinge on whether there is a mode of thinking and speaking about poly-theism available from the Greeks, that is workable for every man and woman and not just for an academic elite of professional philosophers and theologians.

3. Whether there is a viable way of thinking and speaking about our contemporary condition in ancient polytheistic theol-ogy will depend on whether the ancient stories of the gods and goddesses enable us to put a little life, a little feeling, back into Western thinking, which because of its principally rationalistic style has left us with abstractions and logics that do not help us much with our very concrete confusions. So in Chapter Three, we will explore the possibility of re-mythologizing Occidental thought, not so as to give up logic and reason, but to see the pos-sibilities of vital stories lurking in the corners of our ideas and in the depths of our reasonings. In the process of this explora-tion it will be necessary to show the relation between religious thinking in the West, especially Christian monotheistic theol-ogy, and Greek polytheism. What we need to discover is whether Occidental theology is the culprit responsible, not only for the death of the God of its own tradition, but also for repressing the polytheistic pantheon that could be a contemporary resource for social and psychological meaning.

4. If a new polytheistic theology could be a new resource for everyday life, we need to know how, and especially how we will need to conceive of the gods and goddesses so that they may have

a lively effect on our exploded horizons. In Chapter Four, we will probe the deeper meanings of the gods and goddesses in real life by noting a quiet revolution in dynamic psychology and by reporting at length on one of the leaders of this revolution. In this way a polytheistic psychology will be seen to be a clue in the task of re-relating religious explanations to life experiences.

5. In the final chapter, we shall summarize the cultural, philosophical, and psychological aspects of the new polytheism and offer some very tentative but specific suggestions as to the whereabouts of the reborn Immortals, in our culture and in our religious consciousness.

TWO

THE GOLDEN RING AND THE GROWING BLACKNESS:
MONOTHEISM, POLYTHEISM, AND THEOLOGIZING

T he story of how we got to be monotheistic in so many areas of life begins with an argument. Only a few decades ago, a battle raged among theologians as to the relative merits of monotheism as over against polytheism; as to whether having a center means being stable or being hung up; as to whether having a fixed horizon means that one is hemmed in or that one is maturely realistic about the way things are. In order to understand the implications of decadent monotheism—whether in society, in self, or in religion—we would do well to familiarize ourselves with what this tempest in a theological teapot was all about.

The story of the argument begins with a book entitled *Radical Monotheism and Western Culture,* written by the American theologian H. Richard Niebuhr. The essays in the book carry copyrights dating between the years 1943 and 1960, but it is the current paperback edition, published first in 1970, that deserves initial interest. This publishing history is of more than scholarly concern to our subject because of the cover illustration on the most recent edition. It is done predominantly in black with white lettering, and a large, three-quarter-page gold circle brightly circumscribes what appears to be a dark, shadowy, cloudlike nebula, something like a blob of protoplasm or a growing amoeba. The many small oval-shaped blobs inside the circle do not yet quite fill it, but one wonders what will happen when they reach the boundary of the golden ring. One wonders,

indeed, what will happen when professional theologians can
no longer contain in their regal arguments the growing polytheism of a Western culture whose monotheistic explanations
stifle the evolution that was born within the circle of a monotheistic religion. It may be that the argument between the cov-
ers of the book receives its heaviest critique from the artist who
drew the paperback design.

Not that Niebuhr does not acknowledge the presence of a
growing polytheism in our midst. He does so, and in retrospect
we may wonder why his book was not taken more radically as the
announcement of a Nietzschean future. It is rather his reticence
concerning polytheism, and his theological argument in the face
of what he himself sees clearly, that leave us bemused.

Niebuhr defines "gods" as "value-centers,"[1] the principle of
being and value,[2] and the "center of worth,"[3] and then he notes
that we have many such principles and centers. In fact, he argues
that "our natural religion is polytheistic."[4] Certainly Niebuhr is
realistic enough to note that this view will come as a surprise to
many who live in a Western culture dominated by the monotheisms of Judaism, Christianity, and Islam. But though our religious and political institutions are officially monotheist ("One
Nation under God"), our social existence contains many values,
many principles of being, many centers of worth. We give these
"gods" semi-personal names such as Truth, Beauty, Justice, Peace,
Love, Goodness, Pleasure, Patriotism, and so on. Our consciousness has even derived a polytheistic theology or mythology of
our gods, a system of thinking and speaking about these centers

---

1. Richard Niebuhr, *Radical Monotheism and Western Culture* (New York:
Harper & Row Torchbook, 1970), 24.

2. Ibid., 32.

3. Ibid., 118

4. Ibid., 119.

of meaning that claims that they have autonomous power over man's actions.

Niebuhr notes, too, that the pluralism of gods has a counterpart in a pluralism of society and self. What is valuable for us is not the wholeness of our society or ourselves but the many activities that Niebuhr calls "a bundle off functions."[5] This sort of polytheism is no "peculiarly modern problem," Niebuhr thinks, but a part of every period of human history. It is the sort of thing Walter Lippmann described in his *Preface to Morals* when he said that for man "each ideal is supreme within a sphere of its own. There is no point of reference outside which man can determine the relative value of competing ideals." Lippmann felt that man's "impulses are no longer part of one attitude toward life...They are free and they are incommensurable."[6] Niebuhr finds this human condition to be man's eternal situation, a situation he calls "social faith."

None of us, Niebuhr argues, can live without a cause, without some center of worth, be that conscious or unconscious. This is "a curious and inescapable fact about our lives,"[7] which means that all men have some faith simply because they are men. Even atheism, presumably, is a faith that speaks to specific men out of some center of concern. But Niebuhr affirms not only that man is a sort of faith-animal at base, but also man's "natural polytheism," saying that

> beyond the dark powers, the Chthonian deities of the physical life of man, there are our Olympian gods—our country, our ideologies, our democracies, civilizations, churches, our art which we practice for art's sake, our truth which we pursue for truth's sake, our moral values, our ideals and

5. Ibid., 30.
6. Cited in ibid., 31.
7. Ibid., 118.

the social forces which we personalize, adore, and on which
we depend for deliverance from sheer no thingness and the
utter inconsequence of existence.[8]

Realizing this pluralism of centers in life, we dream of integration, of "a great pantheon in which all the gods will be duly served."[9] But this integration of civilization and of personality, in the form of a "hierarchy of values," a fixed circle, forever eludes our grasp. Synthesis of meaning and being is not achieved, because "each god in turn requires a certain absolute devotion and the denial of the claims of the other gods."[10]

Niebuhr feels that this failure leads to a great tragedy. The tragedy of polytheism is that it divides us within ourselves and from our fellow man. But to him an even greater tragedy is the twilight of the gods. Since none of the many centers of worth that supply life with meaning and significance is able to be an eternal source, each god in its turn seems to die. When social causes and the empires of value crumble, "nothing is left to defend us against the void of meaninglessness."[11] Two things should be immediately clear from Niebuhr's account of polytheism. First, it is the opposite of Nietzsche's. For Nietzsche, monotheism leads to the death of God and the specter of meaninglessness; but for Niebuhr, it is polytheism that leads us to this apocalyptic end. Second, Niebuhr's thinking and speaking about religion, his theologizing, takes its shape from a sociological vision. All that he says about the gods is interpreted as having something to do with man's behavior in the social order. The gods are social values; they are principles for being in a world whose central characteristic is seen to be groups of men standing in varying

---

8. Ibid., 120.
9. Ibid., 121.
10. Ibid.,
11. Ibid., 122.

relationships to other men. Even when Niebuhr speaks of the self, it is in terms of man's social roles, a psychological self-definition that is finally sociological. As he sees it, polytheism is a "social faith." The importance of these two aspects of Niebuhr's theologizing will be much easier to grasp if we juxtapose his reading of polytheism with his reticence about that polytheism and his subsequent affirmation of a "radical monotheism."

Radical monotheism is more "a hope than a datum" in the great faiths of Occidental culture. It is customary for many to look back with some nostalgia to the early Christianity of the apostles, to the high Middle Ages, to the Renaissance, or to Puritan New England. We imagine that monotheism was alive, well, and functioning heartily in such ideal golden ages. But these once-upon-a-time worlds were likely as varied, fragmented, and polytheistic as our own time—at least in the experiences of the men and women living in them. Niebuhr finds, as he studies Christian history, "a mixture of the faith in One God with social faith and polytheism." Further, he is not sure that our nostalgia for periods of relative stability in human meaning is a good thing. He thinks it may be symptomatic of a yearning for "the security of the closed society," and the realization of such a yearning would be stifling to man and could bring him under many sorts of bondage.

For Niebuhr, *radical* monotheism means being gripped concretely, in real life, by a single value center. The manifestation of such a faith seizure is neither a closed society nor the principle of such a society; it is, as Niebuhr puts it, "the principle of being itself."[12] This means that a truly radical monotheism is a faith whose origin is not some single reality alongside of other realities, but is some One beyond all the many from which the many

---

12. Ibid., 32.

of everything else derive their being and meaning. This implies that the One of radical monotheism is not finite. It is not identical with the natural or historic order, but is the principle of being and value in which everything in the natural and historic order is rooted.

All this sounds somewhat abstract and remote. Yet for Niebuhr radical monotheism is not an abstract thing. He says that the One of radical monotheism only appears in our history and our lives as "embodied and expressed in the concreteness of communal and personal, of religious and moral existence."[13] He assures us, further, that it is not in the first instance a theory about human and infinite being and then, secondly, a faith. It is first a faith, an "orientation toward the principle of being [that functions] as value-center...whether made known in revelation or always present to man in hiddenness."[14] But it is inevitable, he concludes, that the man of faith will reason about being gripped by a center of value. This means that "rational efforts to understand the One beyond the many are characteristic of radical monotheism."[15] Faith does not wait on theology; thinking and speaking about religion, though inevitable, is secondary to religion itself.

Niebuhr is realistic in noting that most organized religion in the West has been social faith, hence polytheistic. But the religious ideal is a radical monotheism that will "dethrone all absolutes short of the principle of being itself" and have as its motto: "I am the Lord thy God; thou shalt have no other gods before me." For Niebuhr, this commandment sets radical monotheism face to face with the polytheism of our social faith. The outcome of the war is up to us, but Niebuhr does his best to persuade us that

---

13. Ibid.,
14. Ibid.,
15. Ibid., 33.

one after another of the polytheistic gods will let us down; thus the only answer to the problem of enduring human meaning is to ground our being in the principle of value that is radically monotheistic.

But the story I am telling is that of an argument, and Niebuhr represents only one part of it, one side of the argument. His book, *Radical Monotheism and Western Culture,* was an expanded form of the Montgomery Lectures on Contemporary Civilization, which he gave at the University of Nebraska in 1957—though some portions of the argument had been published fourteen years before.

At the same time that Niebuhr was lecturing in Nebraska, the Louisiana State University Press was announcing a new book by the historian of world cultures Eric Voegelin. It is in Voegelin's book *Order and History*[16] that the argument with Niebuhr's view of polytheism is joined. Voegelin's part in the argument will lead us back into Greek polytheism, a subject that will occupy us in more detail presently.

Voegelin traces the demise of the Greek gods, and we pick up his account at the point where Xenophanes is growing tired of the way Homer and Hesiod theologize, that is, he is weary of the way these early Greek poets think and speak about the gods. Especially he finds unsophisticated the human forms and foibles attributed to the gods in early myths. He notes that as long as men create gods in the human image, there will be as many gods as there are men. Xenophanes's recommendation is to transcend this primitive way of reckoning, abandon the anthropomorphic

16. Eric Voegelin, *Order and History,* Volume 2: *The World of the Polis* (Baton Rouge: Louisiana State University Press, 1957), 178–80. See also Werner Jaeger, *The Theology of the Early Greek Philosophers* (New York: Oxford University Press, 1967), 51; and his *Early Christianity and Greek Paideia* (New York: Oxford University Press, 1969), 123.

mythologies and theologies, and recognize the "One who is greatest," the One all men have in common, whose commonness and universality will correspond to the common and universal fact that we are all human.

Xenophanes is most concerned for universality. He wants to overcome the parochialism of local religions and their mythic accounts. He wants to move in the direction of a Panhellenic spirituality, but in order to do this he has to take a step in the direction of universal divinity: One God.

Xenophanes has attracted the interest of many Western scholars, particularly theologians. The reason for this special fascination has to do with what many regard as an early form of monotheism in Xenophanes, a sort of setting the stage for Christianity, just as the monotheism of Judaism set the stage for Christendom's theology of radical monotheism. But Voegelin finds this interest suspect. He feels it may be a backward reading, a trying to monotheize the Greeks, if not to Christianize them. He admits that Xenophanes was a monotheist, but also notes a fact that is troublesome to those who would make him a *radical* monotheist. Xenophanes often speaks of many gods, as well as One—indicating that he was a polytheist. Occasionally he even talks in a way very much to the distaste of radical monotheistic theologians: namely, as a pantheist. For example, Xenophanes speaks of the goddess Iris as "a cloud, purple, and scarlet and yellow to view."[17]

Xenophanes—the conclusion can hardly be resisted—was *at the same time* a monotheist, a polytheist, and a pantheist. Voegelin argues that this will be a problem only to those who think of "the symbolization of divinity," or theology, as a matter of theoretical system-making. If a theologian believes that "religion" is an adherence to a set of propositions, creeds, and dogmas that

---

17. Cited in Voegelin, *Order and History*, 179.

have to do with the existence and nature of God, then he will be forced by his own implicit logic to be decisive about an adherence to one or the other of mutually exclusive systems. If theology is a matter of logic and rationalistic theorizing about creeds and such like, then that logic and rationality cannot simultaneously affirm the existence of one God who is otherworldly and transcendent, another divinity who lives in all nature and yet a third set of many gods who are not quite transcendent and yet not quite immanent.

Assuming for the moment that Xenophanes was not an undiscerning man, we must conclude that he did not think of theology as some highly intellectual task of sorting out rational beliefs concerning the existence and nature of God along the lines of strict logic. Otherwise he could not have been simultaneously monotheistic, polytheistic, and pantheistic in his theologizing. Xenophanes must have had another idea about theology. We will have to inquire into that other old idea in a moment, but first we must indicate the importance of the Niebuhr/Voegelin argument to a better understanding of our new polytheism.

Being deprived of a single center of meaning in a radically pluralistic time makes one feel lost. The backlash effect of this feeling of lostness is to make one grasp for any external center of value that comes along, no matter how superficial. This can take the form of ideological fanaticism about a revolutionary movement, a cult formed around a hard-rock music group, a socialized version of Jesus religion, a dedication to yoga, and so on and on. The intensity of the feeling that can be worked up for these new gods, these social centers of value, lends a superficial religious air to the clutter and confusion of the society's new moralities and rituals. But this social polytheism is felt to be in conflict with some deeper meaning, a single hidden center which the person eternally hopes will "get it all together." So man feels

guilty and inadequate in the face of his experience of plurality
and his loss of a single center. Niebuhr points to this situation.

What is needed to offset the feeling of anxiety and inferiority
in the face of an impossible tension between superficial polytheism and deep monotheism is not a hysterical appeal for retreat to
some lost center, but is rather a deeper view of polytheism. That
is, what is needed is for someone like Voegelin to provide a religious paradigm of a deeper polytheism which does not eternally
war with monotheism but includes it, so that one is able to say
with Goethe, "As a moralist I am a monotheist; as an artist I am a
polytheist; as a naturalist I am a pantheist."[18] Goethe's sentiment
points to the fact that when a man makes a moral decision, in
that moment at least he is indeed operating from the standpoint
of a single center of meaning. But the same man, in his daily life
and through every moment of his behavior, while in the business
of creating the meaning of his life makes use, willy-nilly, of all
the structures of meaning and being symbolized by the stories
of the whole pantheon of gods and goddesses. Goethe's saying,
then, summarizes the simultaneity of pluralistic meanings provided in the case of Xenophanes studied by Voegelin.

The argument between Niebuhr and Voegelin has to do with
whether monotheism and polytheism can exist simultaneously.
If we understand the sides taken in their dispute, then perhaps
we can better understand what is at stake when we feel torn
between our social and psychological pluralisms and a vestigial
nostalgia for a deep single center of meaning and value which
seems eclipsed in our time. The Niebuhr/Voegelin difference
can help us at one other point too. In giving us the lineaments
of the paradox between monotheism and polytheism in the context of our longing for a now decadent monotheism, it furthers
the understanding of how we came to be monotheistic in our

------

18. Cited in ibid.

thinking in the first place. This brings us to a part of the story concerning how we got to be monotheists that we laid aside a moment ago.

The Greeks, who had a word for everything, had no word for religion. Nor did they have a word for polytheism or for theology until very late in their history. Would we want to suggest that the Greeks had no religion because they had no word for it? Or that they were not polytheists or theologizers simply because they did not call themselves by those names? Of course not! But what we might want to say is that the Greeks were polytheists in religion and in theology before they were self-conscious and articulate about these matters, which would mean that being polytheistic is possible without theologizing about it in the way that we in the West have come to think of theology. So what *did* the Greeks think about this business of theology? Certainly they talked and thought about religion—and isn't that what theology is all about? Or is it?

For a couple of thousand years, Greek religion did very well without theology. Then Plato invented it, or at least was the first to use the word *theologia*. Theology as we know it, "the science of divine things," is first mentioned in Plato's *Republic*,[19] where the term may be translated "what is said about the gods." But this translation does not do full justice to Plato's meaning, for he meant to imply a kind of thoughtful speaking about the gods governed by the laws of systematic thinking. This is the way Philodemus,[20] Porphyrius,[21] and Iamblichus[22] used the term *theologia*, also.

---

19. Plato, *The Republic*, 379a.
20. Philodemus, *De pietate*, 48, 72 (first century BC).
21. Porphyrius, *Marcellum*, 15 (third century AD).
22. Iamblichus, *De mysteriis*, 1.1 (fourth century AD).

There is a sense in which Aristotle would be using the term
theologia in a slightly broader way a few years after Plato wrote the
Republic. In his *Metaphysics*,[23] he included Hesiod and Orpheus
as examples of *theologs*, meaning by the word simply anyone who
speaks and thinks about the gods, in no matter what manner.
Sextus Empiricus, Cicero,[24] and Plutarch[25] used the term with
similar looseness. But even in these cases, logical coherence was
demanded of the thinking a theologian would do.

The point of this ancient history of the word *theologia* is that
the Greek term, when it was finally used, was a word that meant
simply talk (*logoi*) about the gods (*theoi*). The word itself implied
neither more nor less. Certainly Homer, who spoke of the Gods in
connection with that agonizing piece of culture-history we call
the Trojan war; Hesiod, who in the *Theogony* tells all the stories
of the gods in mythic fashion; Aeschylus, who wrote the dramas
of the gods in relation to Greek political life; and Orpheus, who
sang the songs of the gods of his cult—certainly all these were
theologians. Their thought was systematic, but it was not theoretical. It was epic, narrative, drama, and song—each of which
was utterly concrete in its imagery. Theology was not yet composed of doctrines, theories, and formal structures of logical
argument; myth had not yet intellectualized itself into dogma.[26]
Precisely the rationalizing, abstracting process in the science of
divine things is what would happen after Plato—after thinkers
had learned their philosophical lessons.

---

23. Aristotle, *Metaphysics*, 983b29.

24. Sextus Empiricus, *Adversos mathematicos*, 2.31; Cicero, *De naturum
deorum*, 3.21.53.

25. Plutarch, 2.421e. See also Karl Kerényi, *Zeus und Hera: Urbild des
Vaters, des Gatten, und der Frau* (Leiden: E.J. Brill, 1972), 36.

26. Gerardus van der Leeuw, *Religion in Essence and Manifestation*,
trans. J.E. Turner (New York: Harper & Row Torchbook, 1963), 560.

There is a sort of fascism about rationalism and intellectualism—a sort of rigid, one-party dictatorship of the mind that forcibly suppresses feelings and intuitions expressed in concrete images and symbolized in the telling of stories. It would seem inevitable that the God of a monotheistic theology would die, that He would suffer an ineluctable demise. The imperialism of the mind, like that of Prometheus's Zeus, cannot forever endure without the resource of life that comes from feeling and intuition. The mind simply cannot account for all of life. By itself it is finally impotent. Thinking monotheistically about the deepest matters of the heart and spirit cannot put man in touch with life as can another sort of *theologia*: the telling of the tales of the gods and goddesses in personified concreteness.

Yet not only is social and psychological fascism a danger lurking in monotheistic thinking, but there is danger in polytheism too, especially if one thinks it, like Niebuhr, in a sociological way:

> On the one hand we can continue... in the direction of what, theologically regarded, is a proliferating polytheism; on the other hand we are asked to submit for the sake of order and peace to some overlordship, whether this be exercised in the name of a nation or cause whose security is valued beyond all other goods, or of a movement that promises to deliver man from evil by five-year stages. Polytheism is as real in reputedly irreligious modern society as ever it was, though now the gods go by the name of values or of powers...The greater the fragmentation the greater is the peril—and the attractiveness—of some monistic organization of study or devotion."[27]

The argument and the warning should be clear as a bell in our time. A pluralistic society, with subcultures, countercultures, generation gaps, and relativized moral codes, is ripe for the next

---

27. Niebuhr, *Radical Monotheism*, 94–95.

overarching ideology that comes along. Any fascism will serve to organize our anarchic social polytheism into a pantheon as long as it is rigid enough, being thereby *apparently* strong, secure, and stable. Certainly this is a real danger.

But the danger of monotheism is equally clear from the story of how we got to be monotheists in the West, even before the time of the prophets of Judaism or the proclamations of Jesus or Mohammed. Monotheism came about in the evolution of a self-consciousness that thought and spoke about itself in a certain way. It is not that all thinking is monotheistic; it is rather that all abstract, formal, logical, and speculative thinking is inevitably monotheistic. As soon as one asks for the essence, or substance, or principle of being behind the diversity and richness of what appears on the face of all life, the question itself leads to a kind of thinking and speaking that eventually will lose touch with reality. And if the gods and goddesses are spoken of and thought of in this monotheistic, one-dimensional, univocal way, religion will not be able to comprehend itself in relation to everyday life, while life in turn will not be able to discover its deep religious dimensions.

Several things may be said at this point:

1. Theology is not what we in the West have come to think it is—at least it is not necessarily the abstract, dogmatic, doctrinal, and credal business of Occidental monotheistic thinking alone. *Any* thinking and speaking about ultimate matters of human meaning and being is *theologia*. The implication is that all men are theologians, and the sooner *professional* theologians learn this, the richer our theologizing will be.

2. A counterpart to this first point is that all men are intellectuals. This is not to say that all men think alike, nor do all men think abstractly and formally. But that all men think, and that many think in ways different from the way others think, means

that thinking is polytheistic. Thinking is at least pluralistic, and insofar as our diverse pluralistic ways of thought are grounded in some deep concern (which is what the gods name), the thinking is not only pluralistic, but is also polytheistic.

It is an axiom in the American heritage that intelligence and intellectualism are not the same. An intellectual is one who goes to the university; but many men who have never attended classes at a college or even a high school are intelligent. In fact our anti-intellectualism in America would suggest that many men who are not intellectuals are far more intelligent than university types, because they are in touch with life. So goes the American theme.[28] But what is felt by many Americans about the dichotomy between intelligence and intellect may simply be an anti-intellectualistic way of saying that all men are intellectuals. This would be the case if we can think of thinking in a polytheistic way, not limiting our view of intellect to some monotheism of American pragmatic ideology or American university education. American intellectuals would do well to begin thinking of all men as intellectuals, disposing thereby of the higher-education mentality that says that a man is only worth something if he goes to college. This is the only way around the monotheism of an opposing view: that a man is only worth something if he gets his hands dirty in the real world as opposed to the ivory-tower world, which is viewed as somehow unreal.

3. The thing that intellectuals and professional theologians can learn from "the people" is that thinking, including thinking and speaking about God, or about the gods and goddesses, is polytheistic. This means that a polytheistic theology that corrects our traditional Western monotheistic theologizing will

---

28. I am indebted to Professor Thomas F. Green of Syracuse University for this idea concerning the dichotomy between "intellect" and "intelligence" in the American *mythos*.

consider the stories of the gods, told in concrete images, to be fundamental to the task of theology. In fact, narrative theology may be the only way in our time to revivify an irrelevant doctrinal theology that has abstracted itself out of life by managing to kill God. Concrete images make for a theology of the imagination and an imaginative theology, as opposed to formal theologizing of a conceptual sort. Placing the concrete images in a narrative adds the dimension of time and temporality to a theology that otherwise offers only spatial constructs of meaning, ruled over by a logic that may be able to tell true from false, but cannot account for what is real, a reality in which truth and falsity, life and death, beauty and ugliness, good and evil are forever and inextricably mixed together. The beauty about stories is not only that they contain many elements all of which are moving in some process, but also that each element has many potential meanings, all at once.

4. Religion means being gripped by a story. The story can be named by an image, and the story of the name can be told through the rhythm of the story's images.

5. One man or woman probably can be gripped by only one story at a time, though the story will have many characters (images) and be in flux (rhythm), which means the narrative is the symbolic expression of a lively process. This translates into the formula that man is monotheistic, insofar as he is gripped by one God at a time; but in order to think and speak about that God, he will have to be polytheistic, since the story may involve marriages with other gods, parentage by still others, offspring of godlings and maiden goddesses. Niebuhr has said that down deep we are monotheists, but on the surface we are polytheists. Voegelin says that down deep we may be monotheists *and* polytheists, whether one rather than the other depends on the degree of abstraction with which we think and speak about the depth.

I am saying that in faith, man is a monotheist, or at least a heno-
theist (that is, worshipping one god at a time in a large pantheon),
but in theology—in which every man participates insofar as he
thinks and speaks of these things at all—man is *necessarily* a
polytheist, given the plurality of life and meaning. To think dif-
ferently is self-deception, a self-deception perpetrated by monotheistic thinking.

THREE

SLEEPING BEAUTIES: THEOLOGY AS FAITH
SEEKING UNDERSTANDING

Little is remembered about Aeschylus's tragedy, *Aetnae,* one of the last plays written by the great Greek dramatist. Only a snippet of the story remains.[1] Talia was one of the goddesses of charm, a daughter of Hephaistos, the smith god who is the master technologist. When it was revealed to Hera, the wife of Zeus, that Talia was one of the many women with whom Zeus had had an affair, the eternally jealous wife set about to persecute poor Talia. Discovering the persecution of his lover by his wife, Zeus hid Talia in the depths of the earth until such a time as she gave birth to two boys, who were called Palikes, a word the Greeks also used to refer to a lake near Leontini in Sicily which had the curious characteristic of emitting two jets of volcanic gas. If you repress or forget the gods and goddesses, they will burst forth from the watery depths in an explosive way.

The same thing happens in *The Sleeping Beauty,* which is a folktale form—the people's version—of an old Greek story about a goddess. When the king and queen have a banquet for their young daughter, one fairy (or witch, or goddess) gets no invitation. But the one who is forgotten comes anyway, uninvited, and becomes the source of the curse that puts Beauty to sleep. Actually, the curse is death, but another fairy (or witch, or goddess) intervenes in it. She cannot do away with death, nor with the

---

1. See Marie-Louise von Franz, *Problems of the Feminine in Fairytales* (New York: Spring Publications, 1972), 9.

forgotten source of death, but she can soften it to a long period of youthful latency during which the princess is not awake to the beauty that all the while sleeps in her. It takes another event, the kiss of the prince (or ogre, or god) to bring new life and fruitfulness to light.[2] It is as if the transformations of history, in our society and in our life, are the contending of the gods and goddesses who become curses of everyday life if repressed or forgotten. The writings of Aeschylus are to the point in another way too. In his famous trilogy, The *Oresteia,* Agamemnon and his son Orestes forget the power of the Furies (or Fates) in everyday life. But on the other hand, Agamemnon's wife Clytemnestra and her lover Aegisthus forget the power of Apollo. The curse of this family called Atreus is that as long as a man or woman neglects the Furies on the one hand, or Apollo on the other, life is tragic. In the third play of the trilogy, *The Eumenides,* the curse is ended, but it ends in heaven (on Mount Olympus) by the power of yet a third sort of divinity, Athena. Athena knows it would be unrealistic in an Apollonian age—an age of increasing complexity in war and political life, an age of rapid urbanization and technology, an age of specialized knowledge and expertise, and an age of heightened philosophical self-consciousness and agonizing reflectivity—it would be unrealistic in such an age not to acknowledge the power of Apollo, for the age is what Apollo is. Yet she makes a place for the Furies—the guardians of close family ties among blood relatives, the chthonic deities of the ecological balance in nature, the upholders of femininity in a time when women are masculated and men are emasculated—Athena acknowledges in the Furies the deep-rootedness of the origin and fate of an Apollonian people.

In another of Aeschylus's plays, *Prometheus Bound,* the title character announces that Zeus will one day die because he for-

---

2. Ibid., passim.

gets other gods and asserts himself as king over them all. He has come into power by rendering his father impotent, just as his father (Cronus) in a former time had come into power by asserting himself over Zeus's grandfather (Ouranos), whose name means heaven itself. But Zeus, by thinking himself free of these other powers, only succeeds in deceiving himself and bringing about the day of his own demise. Prometheus's secret concerning the death of God is that Zeus will one day die of a disease we call monotheism. By repressing or forgetting the gods, which one can only do in the name of yet another, one only succeeds in bringing about the eventual loss of power of that in which one has invested all significance.

We all have Oresteian complexes.[3] This means that as long as we persist in asserting one power over others, we will lose the richness and depth of having multiple resources, but we will also thereby eventually lose even the one power in a traumatic death of God. The clue from Athena is to make a place for them all, when they wish to appear as resources of meaning. The result, of course, will be polytheism. But the function of such a polytheism is to put an end to the curse of the House of Atreus, to put an end to the vicious Promethean and willful cycle of gods (a sort of pendulum action in the pit of our being), and to put an end to the continual sleep of an aesthetic existence that, given the proper kiss, is fruitful, creative, liberated, and (like that kiss) has some real feel to it.

One way to get the feeling back into thinking is to remythologize it, repeople it with gods and goddesses, so that the abstractions take on aesthetic concretion and the ideas may be reinvested with passion. I have pointed out already that the gods and

---

3. See David L. Miller, "Orestes—Myth and Dream as Catharsis," in *Myths, Dreams, Religion*, ed. Joseph Campbell (New York: E.P. Dutton, 1970), 26–47.

goddesses are forgotten when thinkers substitute abstract concepts for their names, and when the stories become transformed
rationalistically into types of formal logic. Images become ideas;
narrative becomes syllogism. To reverse this direction is not to
give up logical thinking or rational discourse. Rather, it is to
become aware of the pantheon parading through our thoughts
without our control and even against our will. It is to put ourselves in touch once again with the deeper dimensions of ideas
and thought, to acknowledge the religious polytheism that we do
not possess, but that indeed possesses us.

In the beginning of Western thinking about meaning and
being, men were still dimly aware of the incipient religious polytheism of their everyday ideas and logic. Aristotle acknowledged
that his philosophical concept of "the unmoved mover," which is
the essence of Being-itself, was nothing more than an abstract
name for what in popular religion had been called the gods.
He admitted, too, that the whole of school philosophy was just
another vocabulary, formal and logical, for what Hesiod had told
in mythopoetic form as the stories of the gods.[4]

If we have managed to get rid of the gods by thinking in a
particular sort of way (that is, monotheistically), and if the concepts, categories, ideas, and logics of that thinking are simply
new names for the gods, then there is a curious twist, a sort of
ironic reversal in the story. We did not get rid of the gods and
goddesses at all. They are still there, as Aristotle knew—repressed
and forgotten to be sure, but actually alive and well, lurking in
our ideas, shadowing our logics, insinuating their stories into
our categories and concepts. We have just pretended we did not

---

4. Aristotle, *Metaphysics* 8.1074a38–b14; B4, 1000a9. See Werner Jaeger,
The Theology of the Early Greek Philosophers (New York: Oxford University
Press, 1967), 12, and his *Early Christianity and Greek Paideia* (New York: Ox-
ford University Press, 1969), 47.

notice those sleeping beauties, and in the process we forgot the stories, which is to say that we forgot that we were pretending. In order once again to remember what we have forgotten, and in order to stop our rationalistic pretense, we shall have to retrace the process of how we came to forget and to pretend. In this way we shall be able slowly to relearn to be articulate in our new cultural polytheism.

What the early Greek thinkers really objected to in polytheism was the anthropomorphic way of thinking about human meaning, giving ideas names, as if the gods were people. This amounted to personifying the matters of deepest concern to man and telling stories about the matters that had been thus peopled. This was Xenophanes's main gripe.[5] But in calling for a principle of unity, whether one god (Xenophanes) or *being* itself (Parmenides), the early Greek philosophers did not escape polytheistic thinking; they just gave it less compelling names and guaranteed that only an esoteric few would thereafter be considered sophisticated and educated enough to be called thinkers (i.e., philosophers). If we were to look closely enough into the ideas, concepts, and categories of sophisticated philosophers of the fifth and fourth centuries in Greece, we should be able to uncover all the gods and goddesses of the polytheistic pantheon. And if we were to persist in our probing, we might be able to delve into these philosophers' logics, the formal structures of their thought, and there discover the narratives, the imagined processes of meaning, in a lively and human form.

All Western thinking may be seen as springing from two impulses and two strategies. The classicist Francis Cornford calls these impulses and their corresponding strategies "scientific" and "mystical." In the beginning, Anaximander is an example of the former and Pythagoras of the latter. Scientific thinking takes

---

5. Jaeger, *Early Greek Philosophers,* 42.

the evolution of Western consciousness from early cosmogonists in Ionia who thought and spoke about the nature of the universe, through a long history of metaphysics to the birth of natural science in the Renaissance, and finally ends in the various positivisms of a contemporary science and technology. Mystical thinking follows a different but parallel route. It begins with the mystical mathematics of Pythagoras, moves counterculturally through metaphysical theologies and not a few heresies (gnosticisms of several sorts), comes to manifest itself in Pietism after the Reformation, and ends in various forms of Romanticism, from some nineteenth-century literatures in England and Germany to men and women fascinated by sensitivity training, Don Juan, the Yaqui sorcerer, and the *I Ching*.

The point of this double lineage of how we think, whenever we think at all, is that it is based, at the beginning, both sides of it, in polytheism.

> There is a real continuity [Cornford writes] between the earlier rational speculation and the religious representation that lay behind it; and this is no mere matter of superficial analogies, such as the allegorical equation of the elements [air, earth, fire, and water] with the Gods of popular belief.[6]

Deeper than any superficial analogies between Occidental thinking and polytheism is the fact that ancient Greek religious images—Gods, Soul, Fate, Law—are the fundamentals of all later thinking, scientific and mystical, even to this very day. These old images have become our notions of substance, cause and effect, matter, and so on.[7] The outward differences between both types of Western thinking on the one hand and polytheistic

6. F.M. Cornford, *From Religion to Philosophy: A Study in the Origins of Western Speculation* (New York: Harper & Row Torchbook, 1957), v.

7. Ibid.

religion on the other, "only disguise an inward and substantial affinity between these two successive products of the same consciousness."[8] Yet when we think about anything we find today that we have lost the sense for the affinity between the gods and the goddesses and our science or our "mysticism." Thus our new polytheism is without a language, a mode of articulation by which it can understand itself. Our science has banished "the vague," but in the process its rationalistic mode has swept away the feeling in the thinking that makes life lively. "The Gods have disappeared; the Soul is reduced to a dust of material particles; in a word, Life has gone out of nature...Admirable as a tool of research...[abstract thought] strikes a chill of horror into men...who will not seek the living among the dead."[9]

Our modern thinking is dead because it lacks the excitement and compellingness that a story can stir in man. Even our various romanticisms are often abstract, strange, and foreign. They lack the earthiness of the old gods and goddesses. But it was not always that way with Western thinking. "The philosophic Muse is not a motherless Athena: if the individual intellect is her father, her older and more august parent is [polytheistic] Religion."[10]

Some examples will make the point clearer. One can generalize and say that behind Anaximander and the scientific mode of thinking is the whole Olympian pantheon of gods and goddesses that Homer conveys to us in epic proportion. On the other hand, behind Pythagoras and the mystical mode of thinking lurk the shades of Orpheus, Dionysus, and the whole chthonic horde.[11]

The impact of this generalization is felt more deeply, however, when it is specified in the case of particular concepts and ideas

---

8. Ibid.
9. Ibid., vi.
10. Ibid., vii.
11. Ibid.

that predominate in all our thought. Behind scientific thinking lies the notion of Moira or Fate. All the Olympian gods and
goddesses comported themselves, as expressed in their stories,
according to that most ancient of all religious notions, Moira. It
was she by whom gods and men alike were bound. But by only a
very small step of the rationalizing and abstracting imagination
the stories of Moira and every Olympian are transformed into
the principle of a universal scientific law to which all nature,
including human and social nature, is bound. It is this natural order that the scientific philosopher is after, and for natural
science following the Renaissance this order is the indubitable
axiom of thinking.[12]

Similarly, just as Moira lies behind scientific thinking, so the
notion of Dike (righteousness and justice) lies at the root of mystical thinking. The Dike of righteousness and justice is expressed
in the stories of the cycle of nature, especially in the myths of
Dionysus and the chthonic gods generally (Demeter and Persephone, Orpheus, the Titans, and so on). What is especially appar-
ent in the Dike stories is a principle that "mystical thinkers" will
come to think of as time. Just as Moira, and her special repre-
sentative Zeus, will come to be called Being by the philosophers,
so Dike, whose expression may abstractly be thought of as temporality, will come to be called Becoming. Cornford shows the
significance of this subtle change in vocabulary in a book called
The Unwritten Philosophy, where he points out how in early Greek
philosophy "the abstract notion of becoming was still merged in
the concrete image of *birth*."[13] So where the polytheist speaks of
the birth of the gods in stories like Hesiod's, stories that con-
stitute a cycle of one series of gods after another, the thinker,

---

12. Ibid., 143ff.
13. F.M. Cornford, *The Unwritten Philosophy and Other Essays* (Cambridge: The University Press, 1967), 41.

already tending toward the monotheism of thought mentioned
in the last chapter, speaks of the process of becoming, the center
of pluralistic values, the process of concretion, and so on.[14] We
can see in the thoughtful interest in cause and effect on the part
of Greek philosophers arid contemporary scientists the old religious practice of speaking and thinking about the gods and goddesses. Especially is this the case in the genealogical stories that
trace in a narrative, mythic manner the coherent plan (Moira
and Dike) of all the Powers of life.[15]

The point I am making is that at first there was little difference between *theologia* and systematic philosophy. Both work
with "doctrines" (*sophidzontai*), but the former does it in a mythical way. I have already cited Aristotle to the effect that philosophers and theologians are doing the same thing; but it is precisely Aristotle, Plato, and other professional thinkers like them
who are the source of repressing a concrete, imagistic mode of
thinking. Aristotle does this by saying that the philosophers
proceed "by strict methods of proof" and those who tell the tales
of the gods do not.[16] What Aristotle has already forgotten is that
those "strict methods of proof" also are the processes whose
proper names are gods and goddesses and their stories.

Aristotle is not the only one who makes a concession as to
philosophy being in fact a thinking about thinking that is rooted
in stories of the gods and goddesses. "Cicero in his *De natura
deorum* and Saint Augustine in the *De Civitate Dei* see the physi-
cists from Thales to Anaxagoras as...only repeating what they
found in their Greek sources."[17] In fact, not only does all Western thinking have its root in Greek religion, but "every system of

14. Cornford, *Religion to Philosophy*, 160ff.
15. Jaeger, *Early Greek Philosophers*, 8ff.
16. See ibid., 10.
17. Ibid., 8.

Greek philosophy (save only the skeptic) culminated in theology, and we can distinguish a Platonic, Aristotelian, Epicurean, Stoic, Neopythagorean, and Neoplatonic theology."[18]

What we see in this story about the early Greek thinkers is that philosophy was originally a way of thinking and speaking about meaning and being that was dependent upon Greek polytheism (1) for its ideas, concepts, and categories, which were once the images of gods and goddesses, and (2) for its formal structures of thought or logic, which were once narrative processes in mythic tales. This of course implies that polytheism lurks in a thinking that thinks itself monotheistic—that is, thinks itself governed by a single principle of being and by a univocal logic that will lead to Truth in the singular. But there is yet another chapter in this old story.

Not only is it the case that thinking is religiously polytheistic at base, but it is widely accepted as obvious, from Saint Paul to the present, that Western Christian theological thinking is Greek at base. Adolf von Harnack and E.R. Goodenough are only two theologians who have taken the trouble to demonstrate what has been axiomatic for an entire tradition. The former showed in his *History of Dogma* that Greek thinking was the most important factor in shaping how Western man theologizes. And Goodenough has more recently demonstrated the impact of Greek thinkers on the ways Jewish thinking has worked, even in ancient times (see his *Jewish Symbols in the Greco-Roman Period*).[19]

"With the Greek language a whole world of concepts, categories of thought, inherited metaphors, and subtle connotations of meaning enters Christian thought."[20] This is obviously already in

---

18. Ibid., 4.
19. Jaeger, *Early Christianity*, 105, n. 2.
20. Ibid., 6.

the Christian New Testament. Paul chose the Greek philosophical tradition as the most convenient form of thinking by which
to communicate the Christian gospel. Greek modes of thinking
and speaking are present in the Fourth Gospel.[21] Certainly, if
there were any doubt about the impact of Greek thinking and
speaking on the thinking and speaking about Jesus, the case of
the Apologists would put final doubts to rest.

The Apologists were second-century theologians whose task
was to interpret the beliefs of the early Christians to a Roman
Empire that suspected these men and women of atheism! The
Christians were called atheists because they did not worship all
the gods and goddesses. The only thing to which the Romans
could compare the Christians was the philosophy of the Greeks.
"The interpretation of Christianity as a philosophy should not
surprise us, for when we stop to consider for a moment with what
a Greek would compare the phenomenon of Jewish-Christian
monotheism, we find nothing but philosophy in Greek thought
that corresponds to it."[22] Had not the philosophers objected to
the naming of many gods? And had not they urged a thinking
and speaking about the One? Not long after Alexander the Great,
many Greek authors, such as Hecataeus of Abdera, Megasthenes,
and Clearchus of Soli on Cyprus, spoke of the Jewish people as
a "philosophical race." What they meant was that "the Jews had
always held certain views about the oneness of the divine principle of the world at which Greek philosophers had arrived only
recently."[23] So the Apologists, attempting "to make a defense for

---

21. See *Die Religion in Geschichte und Gegenwart* (3rd ed.), ed. Kurt Gall-
ing (Tübingen: J.C.B. Mohr/Paul Siebeck, 1956–1962), 3: 840–41, and Rudolf
Bultmann, "Zur Johanneischen Tradition," *Theologische Literaturzeitung* 80,
no. 9 (1955): 521–26.

22. Jaeger, *Early Christianity*, 29.

23. Ibid.

the faith that is in you" (1 Peter 3:15), in speaking to the Romans, adopted the forms of thinking and speaking, the modes of explanation, by which their being grabbed by the Jesus story could best be understood.

Hellenistic culture could understand monotheism by way of monotheistic thinking because it was accustomed to it in the school philosophers. Monotheism had been creeping into philosophical thinking since Xenophanes, and it had crept into theological thinking in Greece too. Karl Kerényi has noted this little acknowledged fact in a recent book on Zeus and Hera. He points out that in Greek religion the key word has always been *theos*. But when one says *theos* in Greek, he inevitably thinks Zeus. Kerényi quotes a famous study by Lewis Richard Farnell:

> Although the figures of Apollo, Athene, Dionysos, and Prometheus are of more importance in the history of external civilization and of the special arts of Greece, no character in Greek religion has such a wealth of moral ideas as the character of Zeus. At times he seems to overshadow the separate growth of polytheism; and at times in expressing the nature of Zeus the religious utterance became monotheistic.[24]

Kerényi calls this the "monotheistic instinct [*Triebe*] in polytheism,"[25] and he links it to the worship of a High God or Dema Deity in other polytheistic cultures.

The point here seems to be, as we have already seen, that one God rules at a time. But that is only part of the point. The other part is that thinking and speaking about religion in the West proceeds by borrowing concepts, categories, ideas, and logic from Greek philosophy. Christian theology is located at the

---

24. Karl Kerényi, *Zeus und Hera: Urbild des Vaters, des Gatten, und der Frau* (Leiden: E.J. Brill, 1972), 4.
25. Ibid.

intersection of Greek thinking, a Jewish apocalyptic situation, a Gospel content concerning the Kingdom proclaimed by Jesus of Nazareth, and a failing Roman Empire.

There should be nothing new or surprising in the story so far. What *is* surprising, in fact nothing short of remarkable, is that nobody has thought to put the two parts of the story together, the part about Greek philosophy being rooted in polytheistic religion and the other part about Christian theology being rooted in Greek philosophy. It would seem irresistible that someone should be drawn to the obvious conclusion: at base, Christian theology is polytheistic. Christian theology is a thinking and speaking about Jesus that uses categories, ideas, concepts, structures of thought, and logic that are ultimately stories of the gods and goddesses. Perhaps the conclusion was unthinkable before now because Greek philosophy had appeared so monotheistic that it seemed somehow OK to use it as a means of understanding the monotheistic faith of Christendom. But what are we to make of the possibility that the only way for a monotheistic faith to attain the understanding it seeks is through a polytheistic thinking?

If you are deeply gripped by a story, so that it becomes a pattern and paradigm for your entire life, it is inevitable that you will think and speak about that story, even if only to yourself. You will theologize. Faith (being gripped by a story)[26] always seeks understanding—as the medieval theologians put it. But it is not inevitable that when you are gripped by a story you will think and speak about that one story in the way that *professional* theologians have: in doctrines, dogmas, histories, systems, and philosophies. Homer was compelled by one story, and then another, and then another, and so on, and he wrote a novel,

---

26. For a more detailed treatment of this idea, see David L. Miller, *Gods and Games: Toward a Theology of Play* (New York: Harper & Row, Colophon Books, 1973), 164 ff.

an epic, a narrative: a story of the stories. Hesiod was likewise seized, and he wrote a poem, a song, a group of lyrics: a song of songs. Aeschylus was also moved, and he wrote a trilogy of plays: the drama of dramatic actions. To tell a story, to sing a song, to enact a drama—these, too, are *theologia*. They are what the people do.

Jewish theology, though reflecting and meditating on a radically monotheistic experience, has often been more polytheistic in its thinking than has Christian theology. On a single point of the law (Torah) there will appear in the Haggadah many *mashalim*: stories, parables, riddles, sayings of the Rabbis. Jesus, too, told many parables ("Indeed, he said nothing to them without a parable"—Matthew 13:34, RSV). But Christian theology has reduced those parables to a few creeds, all of which say the same thing, and then in turn Christendom has reduced the creeds to a system of thought that, in the case of one part of the tradition, is infallible.

What now will happen if we take the polytheism story seriously? What will happen if it turns out that behind those creeds, peeping out from around the corner of doctrines and dogmas, shadowing the formal structures of the logics of first this *Summa Theologica* and then that Church Dogmatics, there are all the gods and goddesses of the ancient world? Certainly it will be no threat to a monotheistic *faith* (even the Greeks could worship only one god at a time). But it may be somewhat radical for traditional monotheistic *theology*. It may portend an important task for a time when the monotheistic theologizing of the Western tradition is not doing so well anyway; it is not helping us to understand the faith that, in fact, works through our lives. The task may be revisionary to the extent that we may want to try to think the possibility of an honest and forthright polytheistic theology.

The words "honest" and "forthright" mean simply that though our theology has thought itself monotheist (Niebuhr), and though its abstractions and logic have forced it into a sort of one-dimensional thinking (like what happened finally to the logic of Greek philosophy), it has all along been polytheistic. There have even been some clues to this effect. The doctrine of the Trinity has been suspect all along of being polytheistic, though now one wonders who the real gods (and goddesses?) are that lurk in that doctrine. Then there is the matter of all those angels and saints, of which the Reformation, a tireless venture in radical monotheism, managed to purge Protestantism. Did not the reformers speak of *sole fides* and *sole gratia*? Saint Paul even spoke of principalities and powers in the plural, but never seemed to wonder about their specific names or stories. Perhaps the system of sacraments is an undeveloped field, fertile with a pantheon of gods and goddesses. The doctrine of the Holy Spirit has long been a pregnant area for discovering incipient polytheism in the tradition. Perhaps that is why the Church has often slighted this doctrine in its thinking. Jesus himself spoke of the *daimones* as Legion. He said that there were "many mansions" in his Father's house. And the Fourth Gospel recalls that he quoted Psalm 82 to the people: "Is it not written...'I said: "You are gods"'" (John 10:34). As the illustrations multiply, there would seem to be another chapter of the story of contemporary polytheism lying well ahead.

It is tempting to jump ahead in this story, from the Greeks and early Christians to present polytheism, neglecting two thousand years of the tale save for a stray sentence here or there. But first we should pose the developing problem as starkly as we possibly can. In order to do that let us ask ourselves a riddle and muse upon this puzzle of Western thinking.

The riddle is simple. It is one that Henri Frankfort, the contemporary historian of ancient Egyptian religion, invented. He notes what we all know but upon which we seldom reflect: namely, that there have been many stories about gods who die and rise again. There is the Hindu Shiva, whose death and rebirth signals a transformation of cultures, as does the death and rebirth of the Egyptian Osiris, and the Greek Dionysus. There is the story of Tammuz in ancient Mesopotamia, whose death and rebirth symbolizes the rejuvenation of the earth, as Osiris's death and rebirth corresponds to the revitalization of a society, and as the Greek Persephone's death and rebirth correspond to the transformation of the self in the individual worshipper at the Eleusinian mysteries. But what is common to all these stories of the dying and rising God is that they appear in the setting of a people who think and speak polytheistically. Only if there are helper gods, gods in the underworld, gods on the earth, gods in the overworld we call heaven, gods of the process of living and gods of the process of dying—only if there are many is the return of the one guaranteed. Or so goes the story.

Now here is the riddle. There is in the history of man one story of a dying and rising God that is not set in a polytheistic context. In fact, the story of the God who came to earth in the form of a man and died on a cross and was resurrected on the third day had as its setting the only culture that overtly resisted the dying and rising God cults of the ancient world. And not only that, but the Jewish setting for the Christian story is precisely a setting of radical monotheism. The riddle is now obvious: How can a monotheistic theology handle a story of a dying and rising God without eventually losing the point in a final death of the God, a modern loss of religious meaning, a contemporary failure of faith on the part of understanding?[27]

---

27. Henri Frankfort, "The Dying God," *Journal of the Warburg and Courtauld Institutes* 21 (London, 1958): especially 151.

This leads us to muse on the two thousand years of thinking that are about to be omitted from the story. The long history of a monotheistic theology that has been deceiving itself
is not being left out because it is well known; nor because it
is abstract, dry, intellectualistic, and dull; it is being omitted
because it forgot the gods in the name of God. The aim here is to
make contact once again with the sleeping beauties—the strong
ones, not the weak and sentimental ones. Or to use a different
figure of speech: the orthodox theological tradition has had
mononucleosis too long, suffering from a life's blood that was
viewed as having only a single nucleus. It has been an infectious
disease, feverish at points, often enlarging lymph glands to the
point where the nymphs were useless, and above all, sapping the
very energy out of the life of faith. Professional theology, like
mononucleosis, just makes one tired.

But why does school theology make one tired in the way
a story, a song, or a drama does not? Certainly it is not only
because we are not sophisticated or educated enough to understand it, though that may often be the case. At the end of the
last chapter I asserted that it is in the nature of Western thinking since the Greeks (including the theological thinking since
then) that certain human elements of meaning have become
lost. We saw that in losing concreteness Western thinking also
loses the touch with life that an image always manages and an
abstract idea never can. We saw also that in losing the narrative
mode (or the rhythm of a song, or the dramaturgy of theater), the
dynamic elements of time, timing, and process somehow fail to
be represented.

Now we can make this point in a somewhat more sophisticated way and at the same time indicate the real seriousness of
Frankfort's riddle. Martin Heidegger has long had a concern for
the loss I am indicating. He sees the problem in his first major

work, *Being and Time* (1927), and in his later essay, *Time and Being* (1962), as linked to the spatialization of thinking that takes place in the first philosophers of Western history. In thinking and speaking about life, one of whose central characteristics is its temporal nature, philosophers immediately faced an enigma. As eighteenth-century philosopher, Immanuel Kant, put the matter: "Time yields no shape." Now if the only words you have to understand life are spatial words—terms like Idea, Substance, Being, Essence—then the only way to talk about life is spatially. But in the process of doing this you lose precisely the temporal dimension of process, the time, the timing of life and of meaning, which like life is always shifting.[28]

Something else happens here too. When temporality is lost in our thinking and speaking about everything (Aristotle spoke spatially of time as a series of "now points"), Being (the philosophical name of everything, or of what lies behind everything) is identified with Presence, the presence of every eternal present. Past and future are missing. Heidegger wants to rethink all this thinking so that Being is always understood in relation to human being in time (*Dasein*) and is not thought of as Presence but as Appropriation, which one might say is Heidegger's term for what by young America is called "relevance."[29]

Heidegger is attempting to rethink thinking so as to get the life back into it. To do that he knows that he must get time back into Being. Therefore he probes Western philosophy to find where, in the name of intellect, this abstracting from life began; and he pursues his research still further to discover another type of thinking, more primary than the rational sort, one that will be meaningful to us today. This he calls "meditative" as opposed

28. Martin Heidegger, *On Time and Being,* trans. Joan Stambaugh (New York: Harper & Row, 1972), see especially Stambaugh's introduction, ix–xi.
29. Ibid., 21.

to "calculative" thinking,[30] and its sources are the stories of the Greek gods!

Heidegger proposes that we think of the Greek gods as worlds, real worlds. They name, and their stories describe, realities of life that will later become the *logos* (the logic) of the philosophers, but are fundamentally *mythos* (the stories of the gods). The "logic" by which all Western men think, therefore, presupposes the *logos* and *mythos* (name and story) of a god. In the course of time, the names and the stories have been forgotten, and then we even forget that we have forgotten and deny that it is gods and goddesses about whom we speak, or better, who speak through our every thought and word. In this way, logic of a rational sort has become an unrestrained dictator in our lives. As one interpreter of Heidegger puts it, "With the precise methods of deduction and abstraction, he [man] builds up the general concepts which enable him to keep under his hand the rich, concrete life that tends to spread apart chaotically after the bindings of *logos* have been concealed."[31]

But now we have lost that *logos* and the god of that *logos* has died. Heidegger attempts to go on by searching new stories, new songs, new dramas, but not new professional philosophies. In his later years he has turned to modern poets who are telling our story, and especially to the poets whose singing (i.e., the drama of whose verse) is knowingly and feelingly linked to the gods and goddesses who have been there all along, though forgotten in the name of one God. As Heidegger has said, "It is the time of the No-more of the gods that have fled and the Not-yet of the god that is

---

30. Martin Heidegger, *Discourse on Thinking*, trans. John M. Anderson and E. Hans Freund (New York: Harper & Row Torchbook, 1966), 53–57.

31. Vincent Vycinas, *Earth and Gods: An Introduction to the Philosophy of Martin Heidegger* (The Hague: Martinus Nijhoff, 1961), 217.

coming."[32] Perhaps now we would want to encourage Heidegger to revise his saying to read: It is the time of the no-more of the god who has fled and the not-yet of the gods who are coming. One would urge this revision even though we have already seen that Nietzsche's prophecy is at hand. Polytheism will not fully be in our thinking and speaking until the gods and goddesses have been named forthrightly. And there is yet much work to be done before we shall realize the full implications of the argument between Niebuhr and Voegelin, the relation between mythology and philosophy, and the riddle of Frankfort. We still stutter when literal-minded people ask monotheistic questions about polytheism. No one has demonstrated this better than the contemporary American novelist John Barth in his book *Chimera*. In that work, some modern Bellerophon, perhaps Barth himself, says,

> Since myths themselves are among other things poetic distillations of our ordinary psychic experience and therefore point always to daily reality, to write realistic fictions which point always to mythic archetypes is in my opinion to take the wrong end of the mythopoetic stick, however meritorious such fictions may be in other respects. Better to address the archetype directly. To the objection that classical mythology, like the Bible, is no longer a staple of education, and that, consequently, the old agonies of Oedipus or Antigone are without effect on contemporary sensibility, I reply, hum, I forget what, something about comedy and self-explanatory context.[33]

---

32. Martin Heidegger, *Existence and Being* (Chicago: Henry Regnery Co., 1949), 289.

33. John Barth, Chimera (New York: Random House, 1972), 199.

FOUR

STARS, SPARKS, AND LUMINOUS FISH EYES:
PSYCHOLOGY AS UNDERSTANDING SEEKING LIFE

> In the absence of an effective general mythology, each of
> us has his private, unrecognized, rudimentary, yet secretly
> potent pantheon of dream. The latest incarnation of Oedi-
> pus, the continued romance of the Beauty and the Beast,
> stand this afternoon on the corner of Forty-Second Street
> and Fifth Avenue, waiting for the light to change.[1]

These words by the mythographer Joseph Campbell contrast sharply with those of John Barth at the end of the
last chapter. They both know the same thing: that the gods
and goddesses are alive and well. But Barth's character stutters
his affirmation, being located in an ancient world that is dying
to be reborn, whereas Campbell's testimony is firm and forthright, being situated in a modern world *post mortem dei,* where
Nietzsche has already announced our future in polytheism. Two
thousand years stand between the character portrayed by Barth
and the intuition of Campbell; these two thousand years I am
now omitting from our study, as already indicated.

Both Campbell, with his mention of dream, and Barth, with
his indication of the relation of the gods to ordinary experience,
give us a clue as to how our story goes on, as if by itself. Depth
psychology, and especially the experience of long-term psychotherapy, has been for many men and women one of the most sat-
isfying ways to "go on" in a world in which the center has lost its

---

1. Joseph Campbell, *Hero with a Thousand Faces* (New York: Meridian
Books, 1956), 4.

hold, and God himself has died and left man without an effective external mythology.

Surely, during the millennia just past, we have accumulated much understanding and knowledge. Faith acquired its understanding, its theology. People acquired knowledge, a philosophy (first a metaphysics and then a positivism) and science enough to hold them for the modern time being. But the understanding that came with the theology and philosophy, science and technology, was not what people really had in mind. It did not lead to life and reality. And so now, for many, psychotherapy reverses the earlier quest of faith seeking understanding. There is no faith left, just understanding. And now man searches for some life, a little reality, and a lot of meaning. If theology is two thousand years of faith seeking understanding, psychotherapy is two thousand years of understanding seeking life.

But what sort of thinking and speaking is behind this psychotherapy that gives new life to our self-understanding? In his books *The Myth of Mental Illness* and *The Manufacture of Madness*, Thomas Szasz has alerted us to the possibility that psychotherapy is in our time a pseudotheology, an ideological philosophy, a sort of new religion for a "mental health culture" in which guilt and anxiety take the place of sin, repression and hang-ups take the place of the Fall, transference and therapeutic release—"letting it all hang out"—take the place of redemption, and so on.[2] Szasz's work makes us wonder what the effect has been on our psyches and on our psychologies of a dominating monotheistic thinking and speaking that gave man a theology irrelevant to faith and a philosophy irrelevant to everything.

_____

2. See his *The Myth of Mental Illness: Foundations of a Theory of Personal Conduct* (New York: Delta Books, 1967), 204 ff., and *The Manufacture of Madness: A Comparative Study of the Inquisition and the Mental Health Movement* (New York: Harper & Row, 1970), passim.

Norman O. Brown, Ronald Laing, and James Hillman have wondered the same thing. Each of these men has been a veritable Martin Luther in the face of psychological orthodoxy and a psychotherapeutic Church, complete with creeds, liturgies, rituals. Brown has revised radically the ways we may understand the theories of Sigmund Freud. Laing has functioned as a revolutionary in existential theories of psychoanalysis. And Hillman is a Jungian therapist whose writings often upset the "true believers" in C.G. Jung.

Brown reverses Freud's dictum concerning therapy. Freud conceived therapy's goal in the formula, "Where id is, there let ego be"; Brown shows that on Freud's own terms it would be more adequate to say, "Where ego is, there let id be."[3] Laing is likewise radical with regard to therapy. Instead of "adjusting" the schizophrenic pathology to a preconceived notion of normalcy, Laing suggests that we be straightforwardly realistic about schizophrenia: it is one of the ways men and women have of being in the world. Therefore it must have a function whose purpose we will discover if we encourage the process of going mad—not resisting, but going the whole way through to whatever may lie on the other side.[4] And so with Hillman. Like Brown, he wishes to reassert the Dionysian aspect of life and the therapeutic aspect of Dionysus. Like Laing, he accepts multiple modes of being human, suggesting that sometimes therapy may lead to fragmentation, not wholeness. Hillman goes so far as to call for an "end to analysis," meaning by this phrase that the way psychology has conceived its own task can be nothing but stifling to

3. See his *Life Against Death: The Psychoanalytical Meaning of History* (New York: Random House, Vintage Books, 1959), ch. 12, and *Love's Body* (New York: Random House, 1969), passim.

4. See his *The Politics of Experience* (New York: Random House, Pantheon Books, 1967), ch. 5, and also *Knots* (New York: Random House, Pantheon Books, 1970), passim.

a people who have already been deprived of richness of meaning by a Western thinking and speaking that is one-dimensional.[5]

But what is especially interesting about these three men is the common step they have taken into a future sensibility. Though they come from radically different schools of psychology, they agree on one thing. Brown says that Freud was right in identifying psychic life as fundamentally polymorphous, having many forms that are already present in the infant and will shape the meaning of behavior and the behavior of meaning in the adult. Yet Brown thinks Freud wrong and thinks him suffering from a Victorian, moralistic hangover when he identifies this infantile polymorphism as perverse. In fact, Brown suggests, polymorphism is not only the beginning but the goal of all psychic life.[6]

Laing is after the same thing when he identifies the source of alienation. He points out that much human behavior is viewed by man as unilateral; it is an attempt on the part of one person to eliminate experience. Existential analysts in trying to establish a therapeutic relationship between two persons are moving in the right direction, establishing a situation in which a person can be helped to experience full personhood. But Laing knows that too often the therapist's preconceived notion of "full personhood" is precisely what stifles an expansion of consciousness with regard to experience. It is unilateral meaning all over again.[7]

Hillman is like Nietzsche. What Brown calls polymorphous and what Laing calls antiunilateralism, Hillman names straight out as polytheism. The story of Hillman's wrestling with the gods and goddesses may help us to see a way out of a Western

---

5. See his *The Myth of Analysis* (Evanston: Northwestern University Press, 1972), Part Three.

6. See *Love's Body*, 243–66.

7. See *The Politics of Experience*, 10

self-understanding, a unilateral and monotheistic bind, a self-accusing moralism regarding our natural polymorphism. It may help us to find a ground in which to plant our understanding of social polytheism (Niebuhr), philosophical polytheism (Voege-lin), and the relation of ancient mythology and philosophy to each other and to our present pluralistic predicament. In short, Hillman's struggle to achieve a polytheistic psychology may give us a way of dealing with our new cultural polytheism. It may provide us with a clue as to how we may go about thinking and speaking about the deepest matters of heart and soul.

Hillman begins by assuming that most understandings of the psyche have in the past been based on a fundamental mis-take of artificially separating "in here" and "out there," sub-ject and object. This mistake can be rectified "by remember-ing that behavior is also fantasy and fantasy is also behavior, and always."[8] This means that fantasy is physical. "We cannot be in the physical world without at the same time and all the time demonstrating an archetypal structure." The corollary to this is that behavior is itself imaginal, symbolic, metaphoric. Freud named one of our many imaginal fantasy structures by the name Oedipus. Presumably this is just the beginning. We enact many myths in the course of our lives. We feel deeply the configurations of many stories. We are the playground of a veri-table theater full of gods and goddesses. What do the gods and goddesses want with us? Our task is to incarnate them, become aware of their presence, acknowledge and celebrate their forms, so that we may better be able to account for our polytheism.[9]

---

8. James Hillman, *Pan and the Nightmare* (Thompson, Conn.: Spring Publications, 2020), 51.

9. See Hillman's "Commentary to *Kundalini: The Evolutionary Energy in Man* by Gopi Krishna," in *Inhuman Relations*, The Uniform Edition of the Writings of James Hillman, vol. 7 (Thompson, Conn.: Spring Publications, 2021).

The psychological advantage of naming the unconscious structures of behavior and feeling by the names of divinities is that this strategy accurately identifies the nature of the dynamics of the psyche. This dynamic works as an impersonal force through our persons. It is not obedient to our ego will power. Further, the dynamic of the psyche is a collective factor, belonging to all men, not just to the personal biography of one. The stories of the Immortals are a joy because they are splendid, concrete, powerful, yet real, personal, full of feeling. The gods and goddesses give to psychological understanding an Archimedean point of leverage on what would otherwise be isolated, anecdotal, biographical meaning. So Hillman notes that

> the psyche has...needs for *impersonal* satisfaction. But until our culture has re-established a harmony with the major archetypal forces within life—the diurnal rhythms and the seasons, the markings of time in biography and the spirits of place, the ancestors, offspring, family and nation, the movements of historical events, and death—in terms of the gods and goddesses who govern the personal, our feeling function necessarily remains in one essential respect inferior, even pathological. For it is deprived by the secular world in which we are set from bearing the values of and connecting existence with archetypal reality.[10]

Hillman develops a view of the self that is like "stars or sparks or luminous fish eyes," a view that seriously subordinates any view of psychology that concentrates on stages (Erich Neumann or Erik Erikson), on the hero journey (Otto Rank), on wholeness and integration (C.G. Jung and Sigmund Freud), or on any other hopelessly " Protestant direction of analytical psychology," such as the panacea of love, the merit of hard work on oneself, a strong

10. "The Feeling Function," in Marie-Louise von Franz and James Hillman, *Lectures on Jung's Typology* (Thompson, Conn.: Spring Publications, 2020), 178.

ego, trust in simplicity or naivete or group process, an anti-intellectualism of childish trust in the unconscious, a pilgrim's progress toward therapeutic fixity, or some other "peculiar combination of introverted religiosity and missionary polarization."[11]

The image of the self implied by this argument makes Babel "a psychological improvement" over a psychological goal that is just a subtle form of an old rationalistic theology "taking prisoner every thought for Christ" (Gregory Naziansus), a theology that, "like Kronos, feeds on the gods it swallowed."[12] Hillman asks rhetorically: "If there is only one model for individuation, can there be individuality?"[13]

This, of course, implies that fragmentation may be the result of therapy and individuation, "each individual struggling with his *daimones.*"[14] Nonetheless, such a polytheistic view of self "reflects more accurately the illusions and entanglements of the soul,"[15] and "without a consciously polytheistic psychology we are more susceptible to an unconscious fragmentation called schizophrenia."[16]

Jung struggled with alternate views of self, for sometimes he spoke more of completed mandala patterns and integrated selfhood, and on other occasions he spoke of the plurality of archetypes. Hillman thinks that when the former obtained in Jung's writing it was an example of a "fading Christianity coming back in the guise of a theology of the Self" claiming "the soul for its own." So "the *imitatio Christi*—no longer a religious

---

11. James Hillman, "Psychology: Monotheistic or Polytheistic?" *Spring: An Annual of Archetypal Psychology and Jungian Thought* (1971): 202.

12. Ibid.

13. Ibid., 200.

14. Ibid., 199.

15. Ibid., 198.

16. Ibid., 200.

dogma or practice—becomes a psychological dogma—now called 'wholeness.'"[17]

Hillman takes some time, therefore, deposing the ruling notion of "first polytheism, then monotheism," as if monotheism were a higher or better stage or state of being. Specifically, he cites Radin's studies and the work of phenomenology of religions generally, against the materials of the *Urmonotheismus* school (Schelling, Schmidt, et al.) and its offshoots (Nilsson and dominant Protestant biblical theology). He does this primarily as a practicing therapist who is careful enough to "giving each god its due," as he himself puts it. "Artemis, Persephone, Athena, and Aphrodite are better than a unified image of Maria."[18] It is not that Hillman wishes to suspend the commandment of "no other gods"; he simply wishes to extend it for each mode of consciousness. "Myths may change in a life, and the soul serves in its time many gods."[19]

In *The Myth of Analysis,* Hillman manages to elucidate the functioning archetypal complexes of the following gods and goddesses: Adam, Anthropos, Aphrodite, Apollo, Ariadne, Artemis, Asclepius, Athena, Atman, The Bacchae, Buddha, Cabiri, Centaurs, Circe, Confucius, Cybele, Daphne, Demeter, The Devil, Dionysus, Diotima, Electra, Eros, The Eumenides, Eve, Hades, Hebe, Hecate, Hera, Hermes, Hypnos, Ishtar, Isis, Jesus, Kama, Krishna, Lucifer, Maenads, Maria, The Moon, The Muses, Narcissus, Nyx, Oedipus, Pan, Persephone, Prometheus, Psyche, Rudra, Saturn, Satyrs, Shiva, Silenus, Tiresius, Wotan, Yahweh, and Zeus![20] And to think, for Freud it was only Oedipus, and for Jung, Christ!

---

17. Ibid., 204
18. Ibid., 198.
19. Ibid., 201.
20. Hillman, *The Myth of Analysis,* 264-66.

Hillman is simply making the point that though we are monotheists ("one god at a time"), a monotheistic psychology will not
suffice to explain the richness of our deepest psychic reality
("in its time, many gods"). Hillman knows from his experiences
in therapeutic sessions that "the revelation of fantasies exposes
the divine."[21] He knows, too, that this means that "in a certain
sense God is dead—but not the gods."[22] And because he knows
these things, Hillman finds that "the effect of the gods on the
psyche is the re-vision of psychology in terms of the gods...The
psyche is thus forced by the gods to evolve an archetypal psychology to meet its needs, a psychology based not on the 'human'
but within the 'divine.'"[23]

Such a view is more radical than that of another psychologist, Kenneth Gergen, though the latter may be feeling for
the same sort of new sensibility. In a *Psychology Today* article
entitled, "Multiple Identity: The Healthy, Happy Human Being
Wears Many Masks,"[24] Gergen challenges two axioms of modern
behaviorist psychology that may have been functioning uncon-
sciously in ways that psychologists might not like if they had
been aware of them. The unexamined presuppositions are: that
it is normal for a person to develop a firm and coherent sense
of identity, and that it is good and healthy for him to do so and
pathological not to. Gergen's point is well taken, but polytheism
is a deeper matter. By contrast with Gergen's social point about
the psyche the implications of Hillman's argument should begin
to be clear. Polytheism is not just a matter of having many roles
in the social order that each individual plays from time to time
in his life. Hillman poses the issue more radically than this, and

---

21. Ibid., 182.
22. Ibid., 265.
23. Ibid., 298.
24. *Psychology Today* 5 (May 1972): 31–35, 64–66.

in the process demonstrates that Niebuhr's view of polytheism, as well as Gergen's is superficial. It is not that we worship many gods and goddesses (e.g., money, sex, power, and so on); it is rather that the gods and goddesses live through our psychic structures. They are given in the fundamental nature of our being, and they manifest themselves always in our behaviors. The gods grab us, and we play out their stories.

This means that the new polytheism is not simply a matter of pluralism in the social order, anarchy in politics, polyphonic meaning in language. The new sensibility is a manifestation of something far more basic. The gods are Powers.[25] They are the potency in each of us, in societies, and in nature. Their stories are the stories of the coming and going, the birth and death, of this potency as it is experienced. Our culture is apparently pluralistic; actually it is polytheistic.

The Powers that are fundamental to our very being are in contention. Marie-Louise von Franz, a Jungian therapist, once wrote, "Complexes are not harmonious in human beings. They can fight each other, and may even push aside other instinctual drives. If a god is forgotten, it means that some aspects of collective consciousness are so much in the foreground that others are ignored to a great extent."[26] Life is a war of the Powers. Man—his self, his society, and his natural environment—is the arena of an eternal Trojan War.[27]

---

25. See Walter F. Otto, *The Homeric Gods: The Spiritual Significance of Greek Religion,* trans. Moses Hadas (New York: Random House, Pantheon Books, 1954), 125–228, and Gerard van der Leeuw, *Religion in Essence and Manifestation,* trans. J. E. Turner (New York: Harper & Row, Torchbook, 1963), ch. 19. See also A. Brelich, "Der Polytheismus," *Numen* 7, fasc. 2 (1960): 123–36.

26. *The Feminine in Fairytales* (New York: Spring Publications, 1972), 25.

27. See the first line of the *Bhagavad Gita,* trans. Juan Mascaro (Baltimore: Penguin Books, 1962), 43.

Our moods, emotions, unusual behaviors, dreams, and fantasies tell us those rough moments when the war is no longer a cold war or a border skirmish, but an all-out guerrilla conflict. These indicators also tell us, by feeling and intuition, when one god has absented himself and another has not yet rushed into the vacuum. We know the war well.

And we know, too, that it will do no good to psychologize the divine. Hillman's psychology helps us to escape from psychologization—paradoxical as that may sound. Hillman is not saying that the gods and goddesses are aspects of my psychological history, subjective dimensions of mankind projected outward onto mythic names and stories. By calling for an impersonal dimension in our psychology, Hillman reaches below or beyond the merely personal and discovers that the gods and goddesses are worlds of being and meaning in which my personal life participates. The transpersonal nature of the archetypal structures performs a "transcendent function" in our life; it gives us an Archimedean point of leverage, a perspective on the world from the standpoint of the world whose name is that of a god or goddess. Hillman's psychology reaches much beyond the subjectivism of most psychologies, and it abhors the supernatural objectivism of most theologies. There is in his manner of thinking and speaking about human meaning a transcendence of both the human subject and the divine object to the point where "in here" and "out there" coincide and supplant each other. By polytheizing his psychology, Hillman provides theology the opportunity to save itself from psychologizing its monotheism.

This all means that something far more important than number is at stake in the question of monotheism and polytheism. Monotheistic thinking will always turn the polytheism issue into a question of the One and the Many. Certainly, part of the polytheistic sensibility is a new openness to multiple forms of reality. But there is something else going on here too. Gerardus van der Leeuw makes the point with a compelling analogy.

> It is absolutely wrong...to conceive the history of religion as a development leading up to "Monotheism." Even for developed religion, concepts like "Monotheism" and "Polytheism" are empty numerical schemes, by which the value of a religion can be measured just as little as can the worth of a marriage by the number of children sprung from it. It is a question then not of the unity, but of the uniqueness, of God: a form like that of God has nowhere been seen by our eyes: with a Will like God's we have never at any time come into contact. Who is like God? The uniqueness of God is no mere negation of his plurality, but a passionate affirmation of his potency...Thus the Monotheism of Islam also was not a protest against Polytheism, but an enthusiastic belief in God's omnipotence...the conviction that all Power belongs to God.[28]

Paul Tillich makes the same point when he says that "polytheism is a qualitative and not a quantitative concept."[29] The quality of a god or goddess is that he or she is potent; he or she is a structure of reality in whose world of meaning and being I am constantly living, or rather, being lived. In our time, as Nietzsche has suggested, the God of a monotheistic way of thinking and speaking has lost its potency, its uniqueness, its power, and Hillman rediscovers that potency, that autonomy, that power in the archetypes of the collective unconscious, the gods and goddesses, about whose reality we must be polytheistic in order to speak and to think appropriately concerning our deepest experience.

---

28. Van der Leeuw, *Religion in Essence and Manifestation*, 180.

29. Paul Tillich, *Systematic Theology*, 3 vols. (Chicago: University of Chicago Press, 1951), 1: 222.

This means that the stories of the gods and goddesses will not be told as long as we tell the story of our personal lives, however unconscious and repressed. The polytheistic tale will not be told, either, as long as we tell the story of our society, culture, history, politics, and ideologies. The stories of history, whether individual or social, may be pluralistic, but they are not yet polytheistic. The stories of biography and nation cannot finally function as deep religious paradigms for ordering man's plural perplexities because these stories come out of the mire of those mortal stories. The stories of the gods and goddesses provide the order in history's story by virtue of being archetypal, which is to say, collective, transpersonal, and transhistorical.

The stories of the gods and goddesses are radical accounts. They populate the structures in which our psychology and our sociology participate, but they are the precondition of that psychology, and that sociology and its history. Psychology, sociology, history—or any form of monotheistic thinking and speaking, be it theological or otherwise—cannot be identified with the stories of the gods and goddesses. They remain who they are, and their stories are constant, though they continually contend with each other in some lively Titanomachia. Psychology, sociology, history—and some two thousand years of theology—may seem to give meaning to man, but finally it is the gods and goddesses and their stories who provide this function.

Hillman does not psychologize everything. He correlates "in here" and "out there," fantasy and behavior, by way of the gods and goddesses, an accomplishment for which all men who suffer a pluralistic time can be grateful and from which they can learn. His psychological revolution does not psychologize the divine, but it polytheistically re-divinizes thinking. It makes possible a re-viewing of two thousand years of that which has failed us. It helps us to see what the gods and goddesses are really up to, what polytheism is really all about, and what is going on in our Nietzschean time. Hillman helps John Barth's character with his stuttering and makes us realize in what sense Joseph Campbell is right in noticing that Oedipus stands on the corner of Fifth Avenue and Forty-Second Street waiting for the light to change: not in Freud's sense, but in some radical way that makes traditional Western psychology and theology obsolete. This, of course, means that there is a lot of new and exciting work ahead, and to that new opportunity we now turn.

FIVE

THE NEW POLYTHEISM:
FIFTY-ONE THESES AND SOME NOTES

The new polytheism has several aspects. First of all, it is a modern sensibility (see Chapter One). This is not the same as saying merely that our contemporary society is pluralistic, nor that our roles are many, nor that our morality is relativistic, nor even that our political ideology is fragmented. These things may well be true, but they are manifestations of something deeper and more fundamental. The more basic feeling is that the gods and goddesses are re-emerging in our lives.

But the new polytheism is not only a contemporary sensibility. It is also a way of rethinking the past tradition of thinking, and especially the orthodox tradition of religious thinking (see Chapters Two and Three). The new polytheism allows us to put together the relation of mythology and philosophy, on the one hand, and of philosophy and theology on the other. The result is seeing a connection between all the gods and goddesses of ancient Greece and an Occidental way of thinking and speaking about religion that we had supposed was monotheistic. The polytheism story tells us something about the present sensibility, and it tells us something also about the history of Western theology.

There is a third aspect to the new polytheism (see Chapter Four). This does not concern modern times nor theology; it is a discovery of the polytheism of the psyche. This works in a curious way: though it is not about our culture primarily nor is it overtly about an outworn theology—nonetheless the recovery of the gods and goddesses of the psyche points the way to the real meaning of our cultural and our theological polytheism. The discovery of the polytheism of the psyche shows us that polytheism is not a matter of some new theology, sociology, or psychology. It is rather a matter of many potencies, many structures of meaning and being, all given to us in the reality of our everyday lives. We worship the gods and goddesses one at a time, to be sure, but they are all at play in our culture and in our thinking and speaking about the deepest affairs of man in that culture.

The new polytheism has three dimensions: cultural, religious, and psychological. A monotheistic background in scholarship tempts the author to try to show how these three different aspects of the polytheism story show modern man a way beyond the religious, social, and psychological confusion of his age. It would be marvelous at this point in the book's argument if the author could generalize on the various aspects of the polytheism theme and come up with a universal proposal for human meaning in our time, a sort of positive, integrated conclusion. But that is just the point: there is no single proposal available now. That was where the explanation systems of Western monotheism failed us—by putting it all together abstractly, rationalistically, pseudomystically, and artificially. Such strategy is essentially contrary to the new polytheism, which simply does not lend itself naturally to theologizing and philosophizing in the monotheistic manner. It is lived in one's deepest feelings.

Thus, instead of coming to a focus, the various lines of thinking in the book at this point explode, fly into many pieces, each one of which is the center of a potential world of meaning. There is no intrinsic order among these various worlds, no necessary relation among them. They are presented here in disjointed form, aphoristically, thesis-style, notes at random, a "rag bag" as the Greeks would have said. Each thesis is meant to be suggestive, provocative, by association implying much more.

The lineaments of a new polytheistic thinking will, at the beginning, have to take a tentative, exploratory form, probing the new worlds that emerge as our old world goes to pieces. The exploration has as its purpose the discovery of the return of first this goddess and then that god, by whose stories we may get a little leverage on our contemporary human condition. The modern-day Homer who attempts to organize our pluralism epically does so at great risk. He may discover, as did the Greek poet long ago, that he has merely set the stage for the next monotheism, complete with fixed center and rigid horizons of Olympic proportions. The task here is more modest. It is to suggest some of the story lines of the pieces floating through our time. The task here is merely a prolegomenon to polytheistic thinking and polytheistic theologizing, these both being finally the same: namely, the fantasizing of the real life in all religions, and the fantasizing of the religious depths of all real life. It is a naming of the gods and goddesses and a telling of their stories, all in terms of human reality.

The massive technologizing of contemporary culture, far from moving without purpose or form, is playing itself out according to the stories of Prometheus, Hephaestus, and Asclepius. Prometheus steals the fire and ends up trapped on a rock, gnawed at by the power he has himself supplanted by his knowledge. Hephaestus is the divine smith, the technologist supreme, who is the bastard of his mother and at a total loss for sensuousness and feeling. Asclepius, as Pindar says, is the technologist of the feelings; he is the psychotherapist whom technology and its civilization will make into the high priest of a mental health culture.

The desire for political and personal control that plagues the impotent will of society and self, and gives rise to the fantasies of Skinner boxes and electronic manipulation of the aggression- and pleasure-centers of man's brain, is Apollo remembering his youthful adventures with his sister, Artemis, how they ran not only Delos and Delphi, but also everyone they met. Apollo had to suffer unmentionable humiliation for this willful phase of his adolescence by cleaning the excrement from the sheepfolds of King Admetus.

The political and social backlash into a quiet and brooding conservatism, as well as the nearly epidemic nature of psychological depression,follows the pattern of Cronus's story. These aspects of our pluralism show themselves in their Saturnine quality. The story gives away the rhythms such things follow. Cronus was who he was because he swallowed his own children. He lived off what he himself produced, never allowing his creativity a life of its own.

Our apathy, both of youth and age, is Hestia. This is a complex matter, since Hestia is very old, the goddess of the hearth, the fire at the center of the family. But when Dionysus comes, Hestia draws back, retires, goes away in the face of radical madness.

Hera knows the story of the social science takeover in a culture. She knows how computer and statistical procedures come to be revered as true wisdom, how consultants and experts must attend every decision in business and government. She tried to socialize Mount Olympus. Were we to study the story of her failure, we might have deeper insight into social engineering in our own time.

The military-industrial complex is Hera-Heracles-Hephaestus. The formulation of this sentiment is by James Hillman; but its reality is truly lived by us all in some modern version of classical Greek structures.

Activism—whether in the form of altruistic do-good-ism or revolutionary movements—*is the work of Heracles.*

Urbanization bears the imprint of Athena. And when it disintegrates into street riots and muggings, it forgets that Athena, too, had to make a place for the Furies.

The ever-presence of outbreaks of the irrational—in the violent forms of Vietnam or rape on college campuses, or in the subtler forms of compulsive participation in mystical movements and black magic groups—*is the work of Pan,* whose ever-presence made him deserve the name that means "All."

Such are some of the dimensions of our polytheism. There may be more understanding for our cultural crises in the stories of the gods and goddesses than there is in all the social and political theorizing put together. Or, more likely, the diversity in social and political theorizing can also be seen more compellingly through the myths of the Greeks. Suffice it to say that our plurality is radical, so much so that the gods of plurality itself—*Dionysus, Hermes, and Pan*—seem to be loose in our midst.

The mention of these three makes possible a demonstration of the truly radical nature of polytheistic thinking. Pan will do for an illustration. Sex and violence, as characteristic of our time, will do for instances.

Violence takes many forms in itself Pan, Athena, Ares, and Artemis/ Apollo. The Greeks were not content to combine all forms of aggression under one abstract noun. They had several stories that differentiated the many faces of violence. Athena was protectress of the city; she fought defensively. Her style of warfare was not that of Ares, who loved to fight for its own sake. But even Ares was Olympian in his procedures, never so earthy and irrational as Pan, whom the soldiers invoked for a lucky moment in battle. Artemis and Apollo, as I have said, were an adolescent team with none of the sophistication in violence that characterized both Athena and Ares. Furthermore, Apollo would suffer sufficiently to outgrow his violent nature, but Pan—well, it is just his nature to romp down the mountain violating everything in his way!

But Pan is sexual too. *Along with Aphrodite, Eros, and Hermes, Pan teaches us the variousness of our sensuality.* Aphrodite is the love object. Her love is characterized by a compulsion from the side of the lover, whereas her son, Eros, finds his compulsion within, driving him instinctually toward the object. Aphrodite is the woman's body that turns the man's head without his thinking; she is the Playmate of the Month. Eros is the drive to buy Playboy magazine in the first place. Hermes is the love that comes by luck, or as we say, "at first sight." Whereas Pan is rape—the coming together of our sensuality and our irrational violence.

Not only does polytheistic thinking give us impersonal and collective leverage on life's pluralistic meaning through stories of the gods and goddesses, but it helps us to differentiate the polytheistic quality of each of the aspects of our plurality. This gives polytheistic thinking not only a breadth for our pluralisms but also a depth, a resonance, a religious quality that is characterized by its transcendent function.

We may well ask what the pleroma of wide worlds and their expression in the form of polytheistic religion have to do with traditional monotheistic theology, especially the orthodox Christian variety. I have said that monotheistic theology has all along been polytheistic at base. Perhaps some concrete examples will suggest—tenuously to be sure—the association between the polytheism of our new secular experience and the same gods and goddesses hiding in one old form of religious thought. As before, these figments and filaments remain feelings and intuitions concerning many stories yet to be told.

Trinitarian theology is Hesiod's Theogony *in thinly veiled disguise.* Hesiod's recounting of the divine process that moves from Ouranos and Gaia to Cronus and Rhea to Zeus and Hera is the prefiguration of the processionism of the Nicene and Apostle's Creeds, from Father to Son to Spirit.

The ransom theory of the Atonement is an explanation that repeats abstractly the negotiations between Zeus and Prometheus. The power-transaction metaphors give away the whole story.

The satisfaction and penal theories of the Atonement smack of the Trojan War *epics.* The clue is in the sacrifice of Iphigenia by her father, Agamemnon, and in the custom of looting linked to the divine order of the gods.

The moral influence and governmental theories of the Atonement shadow the stories of Athena, especially the stories dealing with her fight with Poseidon over the Acropolis. The governors and guardians of the social order always tell the same story.

The sacramental theology of the traditional Church suggests to the polytheist the Eleusinian mysteries and the whole mythology of Demeter and Persephone.

The theology of creation that would account for the place of nature in the redemption process is ruled over by Pan and many, many others whose names are celebrated in The Homeric Hymns.

Soteriology—the various doctrines of salvation—all suggest the story of the god of variousness whose salvific function is well known in the Orphic cult His name is Dionysus. He is, as Kerényi says, the "archetype of indestructible life." And his indestructibility is interpreted in a story whose "logic" is always a story of death and resurrection.

Eschatology is the domain of Hermes, the thief and trickster, who is psychopomp and mystagogue. Did not Jesus say that the Kingdom comes like a thief in the night?

The theology of the Church (ecclesiology), which is so disparate in fragmented Christendom, has many gods: Hestia, Hera, Artemis, and—in some communitarian sects—Aphrodite.

The doctrines of justification and sanctification are realized and in fact real in the myths of Orpheus and Asclepius.

Christology has had so many Gods empowering its logics that it is difficult to think of them all: some should be named Athena, Dionysus, Orpheus, Hermes, Persephone, Poseidon, Hades, and Hephaestus.

And can anyone doubt that *the doctrine of God is the work of Zeus?*

This is just the beginning. Much polytheistic theology needs to be done before we discover what hides, well repressed and easily forgotten, in the logics of our Occidental theology. The work is not to find allegorical typologies; it is not to make clever associations between far-fetched correspondences. Nor is the work historical: a genetic tracing of the connections that exist in the conscious evolution of thinking, from mythology to philosophy to theology. The first task would be trivial; and the second, even were it possible, would be irrelevant to our purpose. The real task is a far more difficult one, which cannot be satisfied by some academic chore, however brilliantly performed, even were the effort worth it. The task rather is to rediscover the stories of the gods and goddesses, the theology of the people. It is to recover the varieties of religious experience lurking in the varieties of theological experience. The task begins in feeling and intuition, rather than in thinking. It probes the deeper functions of our Western philosophico-theological logics to discover the multi-faceted richness lying in wait for the princely kiss of feeling. The task of a polytheistic theology will not be even begun until there is a sense for life in theology, a liveliness in understanding, a passion in thinking, a love of the gods and goddesses.

A polytheistic theology will attempt to recover the whole pantheon residing in our so-called monotheistic theological tradition.

A polytheistic theology will be a phenomenology of all religions. It may be that the works by Mircea Eliade and Gerardus van der Leeuw are clues as to the future shape of a polytheistic theology. A truly polytheistic theology would be the first theology of religions.

A polytheistic theology will be a religious phenomenology of all culture. William Irwin Thompson (*At the Edge of History*) and Theodore Roszak (*The Making of a Counter Culture*) have begun to help us with this task of naming the gods and goddesses of a resacralized world.

A polytheistic theology will be neither another theism nor another logic. Understanding by way of positing theistic systems and by way of intellectualistic modes of knowing is already monotheistic: it is the imperialism of the mind over the feelings and the will. Polytheistic psychology is always multivalenced, never bipolar, never good versus evil, right versus wrong, finite versus infinite, light versus dark, up versus down, in versus out. There is no orthodoxy in polytheistic theology.

A polytheistic theology will be stories of the gods (rather than theistic systems) *and an aesthetic creation* (rather than a logic of life).

It will be *theopoiesis* (Stanley R. Hopper). Yet one can imagine its relation to recent Christian theology.

A polytheistic theology will be a theology of the word (Karl Barth), *but in the manner of Hermes, who is appointed messenger of the gods because he promises never to lie, but adds that it may be necessary for him not to tell the truth in order that he may not lie.* Hermes was a trickster.

A polytheistic theology will be a theology of culture (Paul Tillich), but in the manner of Dionysus, whose method of correlating religion and culture, sacred and secular, infinite and finite, is by leaving Olympus after reconciliation with his father Zeus and meeting his mother Semele in the depths of the house of Hades. Dionysus's boundary situation is maintained realistically by the ego-transcendence of drunken madness.

A polytheistic theology will be a theology of hope (Ernst Bloch), *but in the manner of Penelope, Demeter, Aphrodite, Hestia, Clytemnestra, and the many others who know hope from the side of radical waiting,* and therefore show hope's many future faces.

A polytheistic theology will be a political theology (Jürgen Moltmann), *but in the manner of Athena, whose clue to reconciliation in the* polis *of Athens is calling on the deity Holy Persuasion, who is not merely rhetoric but whose name* (Peitho) *in its passive form means acceptance.*

A polytheistic theology will be a feminine theology (Rosemary Reuther), but in the manner of all the goddesses—the thousand daughters of Oceanus and Tethys, to name only a few. By being many, these goddesses avoid a monotheistically chauvinistic view of the feminine.[1]

---

1. For an attempt to see psychology's function *vis-à-vis* theology, an attempt that overtly aims at a recovery of the numinous, the imaginal, and the

A polytheistic theology will be iconoclastic (Gabriel Vahanian), *but in the manner of Prometheus chained to a rock with an eagle gnawing at his liver. An iconoclasm is a vital response to oppressive monotheism.*

A polytheistic theology will be radical (Thomas J. J. Altizer and William Hamilton), *but in the manner of the Furies, whose bloody, radical feminineness is transformed by every Athena into gracious goddesses, the Eumenides.*

A polytheistic theology will be juxtapositional and comic (Harvey Cox), *but in the manner of Pan, who brings laughter to Zeus—not to men. Pan brings panic to men, who try to laugh it off.*

A polytheistic theology will be secular (Dietrich Bonhoeffer and William F. Lynch), *but in the manner of the Apollo who presides over the Olympian games.*

A polytheistic theology will be a remythologizing of the tradition (Rudolf Bultmann), *but in the manner of Orpheus and Asclepius, who knew how to tell a story so that it brings life.*

A polytheistic theology will be dancing and playful (Sam Keen and Robert Neale), *but in the manner of Silenus, who teaches Dionysus, and not in the manner of Dionysus, who is responsible for the death of Orpheus and his song.*

A polytheistic theology will be existential (John MacQuarrie), *but in the manner of Oedipus and Orestes, whose tragedies transcend the tragedy of the death of a god by way of the rebirth of the gods.*

A polytheistic theology will be gnostic (Hans Jonas), *but in the manner of the secret knowledge of Hermes, not willful Prometheus.*

---

feminine in a remythologization of theology, see Ann Belford Ulanov, *The Feminine in Jungian Psychology and in a Christian Theology* (Evanston, Ill.: Northwestern University Press, 1972).

A polytheistic theology will be body-conscious (Norman O. Brown), *not in the manner of Aphrodite's Helen but in the manner of Aphrodite's son Eros, who forsakes Aphrodite for Psyche.*

A polytheistic theology will be a theology of the spirit (Nicholas Berdyaev), *but in the manner of Psyche, whose wings are those of the multihued butterfly that has long since sloughed off the cocoon as home only for a worm.*

A polytheistic theology will be a theology of story and narrative (Michael Novak, Stephen Crites, John Dunne), which means that the first task of a polytheistic theology is to learn the stories, all of them.

A polytheistic theology may be analytic (Paul Van Buren), *but in the manner of Apollo, who when he grows up says that in order not to get anything in excess one ought start by knowing oneself.*

A polytheistic theology will not be a fad, but is a name that accounts for all the fads in theology and in culture. It worships all the gods, not men.

Some may think that this book on polytheism has a severe headache, a sort of mental cramp from a Western monotheistic hangover. That is, some may think the point of all this talk about polytheism is an attempt to "get it all together" in the name of some new monotheism that happens to be called by the name "polytheism." The contrary is the case. Polytheism in this book is the name given to disparateness in symbolic explanation and in life, and if it is a viable description of where things are and where they are going, it should have the function of keeping it all apart. It's another way of saying 'I'm not OK—you're not OK—and that's OK" (Sheldon Kopp).

Our life is polytheistic; it is a many-splendored thing, down deep, if we only knew it. Perhaps this is the meaning of the plea that Symmachus addressed to Saint Ambrose when defending the heresy of polytheism against the latter's orthodoxy of monotheism: "The things of heaven and earth are such a wide realm that the organs of all being together only can provide comprehension."

A polytheistic theology, because it makes contact with the immediacy of life out of the depths, *is itself a religion with no scripture, but with many stories.*

A polytheistic theology will release man into depth. He may now trust that breadth in life will be accounted for by all those others who are living the forms of other gods and goddesses. He will be relieved from a Puritan sense of duty to perfection and completeness. He will experiment, first with this god and then that goddess. He will return to the gods who have been forgotten and repressed. And there he will find the depth that has been hiding all along. But because he finds the depth, his return to the gods will not have been regressive, which would mean a return to a fixed single point. The return to the gods and goddesses will be more like a re-turn, as Giambattista Vico or James Joyce would have said, a turning in that circle whose horizons are open to infinity and whose center, since it is everywhere, is multiple. It will be a new turning, no longer vicious but now relieving and liberating. Perhaps it will be something like what Friedrich Schelling felt when he said: "Polytheism…is the way to truth, and is thus truth itself."[2]

---

2. F.W.J. Schelling, "Introduction to the Philosophy of Mythology," in Burton Feldman and Robert Richardson, *The Rise of Modern Mythology 1680-1860* (Bloomington: Indiana University Press, 1972), 327.

Was not Schelling in this sentiment turning to what once upon a time was a very familiar story? Did not Thales say that "everything is full of gods"? And did not Euripides close his most famous play, *The Bacchae*, with the words, "Many are the shapes of things divine"? This may be our story, too, deep down, were we able to acknowledge it. That acknowledgement, entailing a touch with the depths, would be a new turn, a re-turn, to polytheism.

THE LAUGHTER OF THE GODS

No story is the whole story. It takes many stories to tell the whole story, yet the whole is known always and only through the many. Neither is this book the whole story. Much besides two thousand years of history has been omitted, some of it intentionally and doubtless some unintentionally. But the intentional omission is for the sake of the book's story, just as Bob Hope "forgets" to include some details for the sake of the laugh in the joke he is telling.

Laughter is indeed one of the aims of this book—not literal laughter so much as the liberation that comes from a comic release, or, in a Shakespearean tragedy, from comic relief. But laughter is only one of the aims, and at the end we can now indicate some other purposes that have been important in the telling.

1. A certain kind of recent theologizing, one that began about 1918, has had an axiom working in it that has gone unchallenged: namely, that the Judeo-Christian symbol-system of meaning has little or nothing to do with the Greeks. Just as the Jewish people resisted the cults of Baal in Canaan, so certain theologians have been resistant to the Greeks, saying that Greek concepts of religion stood in polar opposition to Christian ideas. In order to claim this distinctiveness of the Christian gospel, professional theologians have had to engage in some silly strategies. For example, in the matter of life after death, theologians have been eager to affirm the distinctiveness of the so-called Christian view of the resurrection of the body over against the so-called Greek

view of the immortality of the soul. Much has been made of this distinction in professional circles. The Christians have never believed in Greek immortality; theirs is a unique view of resurrection. But in order to make this contrast, theologians have in this case, as in so many others, compared the most sophisticated of Christian theologizing with perhaps the most decadent of religious thinking in the Hellenistic world. Actually, the view of the resurrection of the body is well-known in the religious consciousness of certain Greeks; and many believers in Christ would find it something of a shock to hear they do not and cannot believe in immortality. The distinctions between Athens and Jerusalem can be maintained only if the worst of Greek thought (or at least the latest in Hellenistic philosophizing) is compared with the most pristine Christian thinking of the Fathers. It is one of the aims of this book to call professional theologians to be as sophisticated and differentiated in their thinking about Greek religious consciousness as they are about the faith they are supposedly defending. It is time for Christian theology to stop taking its clue from Plato and Aristotle and to begin taking it from where Plato and Aristotle got theirs. Let us stop comparing rotten apples with plump pears.

It cannot be regarded as rank heresy purely and simply to call attention to the importance of the Greek gods and goddesses for Western consciousness of meaning. Not that heresy is a concern. But if it were, there is an interesting precedent for a renewed interest in "pagan" things. Saint Augustine, in his book *On Christian Doctrine*, points out that God himself commanded the Hebrew people to notice that the Egyptians possessed ways of life that should not be left behind, but that the Israelites should adopt and take along (Exodus 3:22, 11:2; 12:35).[1] He felt that by analogy this warranted theology's borrowing from the

---

1. Saint Augustine, *On Christian Doctrine* (New York: Liberal Arts Press, 1958), 75.

Greeks, and he used such reasoning as a part of his own adoption of Greek modes of thinking and speaking about the Christian religion.

2. It was such reasoning that the Renaissance Magus was engaged in when he unveiled "the pagan background of early Christianity."[2] This is a second theme of this book. Certainly a few scholars (for example, Hugo Rahner[3] and E. R. Goodenough[4]) have worked to show the relation between the myths of ancient Greece and Christian meaning, but these few have limited their works to an examination of Christian preaching, in which the gods and goddesses are sermon illustrations for the one true God who is revealed in the life and teachings of Jesus. This is not what I have in mind. The gods and goddesses are not cute allegories and analogies, figures of speech for evangelizing and moralistic orators, just as they are neither psychological nor social roles. Rather, they are the empowering worlds of our existence; the deepest structures of reality.

It is not so much that I have in mind a new program for Christian theology. Christian theology will do what it wants to do, just as it always has. It is rather that one would like to open the possibility of a new way of seeing everything that theologians think and say—and not only professional theologians, but also everyone who thinks and speaks about the deepest matters of life. This way of seeing is through the eyes of the gods and goddesses of ancient Greece—not Egypt, not the Ancient Near East, not Hindu India, not Ancient China or Japan. Greece is the locus of

---

2. See Frances A. Yates, *Giordano Bruno and the Hermetic Tradition* (New York: Random House, Vintage Books, 1969), 2. Also Jean Seznec, *The Survival of the Pagan Gods* (Princeton, N.J.: Princeton University Press, 1972), passim.

3. See Hugo Rahner, *Greek Myths and Christian Mysteries* (New York: Harper & Row, 1963), passim.

4. See above Chapter Three, n. 19.

our polytheism simp y because, *willy-nilly*, we are Occidental men and women.

3. But this book has had aims that are not so explicitly theological. One of them is simply to take another look at the contemporary sensibility in a way that will help release us from the Puritan sense of continued duty that makes us feel that we must "get it all together." We had hoped to point to the possibility that "keeping it all apart" is a safe, a realistic, and an exciting way to "go on." The book aims at a feeling of release.

4. It also aims at the articulation of an intuition about ourselves: namely, that we have been monotheistic in our consciousness, not only in our faith (where one God at a time is not only OK but inevitable), but also in our thinking and speaking about our society, ourselves, our politics, our history, and our very being and meaning. The book aims at a further intuition, too, learned from Nietzsche; namely, that at base we are such beings that only a polytheistic consciousness will account realistically for our lives, and that such a polytheistic consciousness is emerging on the tips of our newest sensibilities.

5. This means also that we aim at a new function for the old gods and goddesses, those sleeping beauties. We have a hunch that they and their stories can open our eyes to a new way of seeing the multiple dimensions of everything. But they can perhaps do more. The gods and goddesses may also teach us a new tolerance—even more, an acceptance of the variousness of ourselves and others. These stories from Greece may also show us, not only a new way of seeing what we formerly called by the negative term "fragmentation," but also a new way of sensing a potency in the diversity and plurality of our modern existence. The book aims at an affirmation.

6. And finally, it aims at a humility of sorts. Not the kind we are proud to possess. But a humility that comes from seeing, with

James Hillman, that polytheism is really all about something very deep. The gods and goddesses are functioning so profoundly that they cannot be accounted for by superficial explanations such as the following: that the gods and goddesses are simply our repressed biographical data; that they are merely metaphors for artists and poets; that they are rhetorical illustrations and anecdotes that help make sermons and political speeches seem more palatable and more learned; that they are forgotten aspects of history; that they are parts of a decayed civilization and a former institutional religion. None of these explanations of polytheism will do. They lead us to the wrong stories.

The stories that must be told are not the ones of Judaism and Christianity. These stories are a part of our history and our biography. They account for social and psychological reality in some real, but surface, way. The stories of the Greek gods and goddesses, precisely because they are not a part of our remembered history or our dim biography, are playing a more radical role in our lives. Sam Keen is right in his book *To a Dancing God*: "The Death of God is the death of storytelling."[5] It is the death of the telling of superficial stories, those stories that form the surface of our lives. But the death of God is also not the death of some more basic stories; it is the opposite. It is the possibility of the rebirth of deeper stories. And precisely this calls for a humility that we may not find possible.

The humility we are called to is indicated by Stephen Crites when he says "the sacred story...cannot be directly told." He goes on to say,

> But its resonances can be felt in many of the stories that are being told, in songs being sung, in a renewed resolution to act. The stories being told do not necessarily speak of gods in any traditional sense, yet there seem to be living

---

5. Sam Keen, *To a Dancing God* (New York: Harper & Row, 1970), 82–105.

continuities in this unutterable story with some of the sacred stories of the past.[6]

Perhaps if we are patient enough, if we listen closely enough to the moods, emotions, unusual behaviors, dreams, and fantasies of ourselves and our societies, we may hear some songs that are very old, now coming once again from the severed head of Orpheus that floats in every sea just off every isle of Lesbos. The songs, their narratives and their dramas, are those of the gods and goddesses announcing an expanding consciousness, a new sensibility, a new polytheism, a remythologization of life.

Nietzsche heard the song and he reported it to us in advance. We began with his prophecy; it is appropriate that we end with his singing.

> For the old gods, after all, things came to an end long ago; and verily, they had a good gay godlike end. They did not end in a "twilight," though this lie is told. Instead: one day they *laughed* themselves to death. That happened when the most godless word issued from one of the gods themselves— the word: "There is one god. Thou shalt have no other god before me!" An old grimbeard of a god, a jealous one, thus forgot himself. And then all the gods laughed and rocked on their chairs and cried, "Is not just this godlike that there are gods but no God?"[7]

---

6. Stephen Crites, "The Narrative Quality of Experience," *Journal of the American Academy of Religion* 39, no. 3 (September 1971): 311.

7. Friedrich Nietzsche, *Thus Spoke Zarathustra*, trans. Walter Kaufmann (New York: Viking Press, 1966), 182.

APPENDIX

PSYCHOLOGY: MONOTHEISTIC OR POLYTHEISTIC?

by JAMES HILLMAN

I

In the conclusion to his late work, *Aion*, heavily preoccupied with Christian symbolism, Jung writes: "The anima/animus stage is correlated with polytheism, the self with monotheism."[1] Although he pays high respect to the "numina, anima and animus"[2] and conceives the self as a conjunction, he nevertheless also implies that as anima/animus is a pre-stage of self, so is polytheism a pre-stage of monotheism. Moreover, the self is "the archetype most important for modern man to understand."[3]

The preference for self and monotheism presented there strikes to the heart of a psychology that stresses the *plurality* of the archetypes. (Archetypal psychology begins with Jung's notion of the complexes whose archetypal cores are the bases for all psychic life whatsoever.) A primacy of the self implies rather that the understanding of the complexes at the differentiated level

---

Originally published in *Spring: An Annual of Archetypal Psychology and Jungian Thought* (1971). Revised and reprinted in *Archetypal Psychology*, The Uniform Edition of the Writings of James Hillman, vol. 1 (Putnam, Conn.: Spring Publications, 2004).

1. *Collected Works of C.G. Jung*, trans. R.F.C. Hull, 20 vols. (Princeton, N.J.: Princeton University Press, 1953–79; *CW* hereafter, cited by paragraph number), 9.2:427.

2. Ibid., 425.

3. Ibid., 422.

once formulated as a polytheistic pantheon and represented, at its best, in the psyche of Greek antiquity and of the Renaissance, is of less significance for modern man than is the self of monotheism. Were this all, archetypal psychology would be nothing but an anima fantasy or an animus philosophy. Explorations of consciousness in terms of the gods—Eros and Psyche, Saturn, Apollo, Dionysus—would then be only preliminary to something more important: the self. The self archetype would be paramount, and one should be investigating its phenomenology in the *quaternio*, the *conjunctio*, mandalas, synchronicity, and the *unus mundus*. The question "polytheism or monotheism" represents a basic ideational conflict in Jungian psychology today. Which fantasy governs our view of soul-making and the process of individuation—the many or the one?

The very sound of the question shows already to what extent we are ruled by a bias toward the one. Unity, integration, and individuation seem an advance over multiplicity and diversity. As the self seems a further integration than anima/animus, so seems monotheism superior to polytheism.

Placing the psychological part of this question to one side for the moment, let us first depose the ruling notion that in the history of religions or in the ethnology of peoples monotheism is a further, higher development out of polytheism. Radin devoted a monograph to this subject.[4] He concluded: "...as most ethnologists and unbiased students would now admit, the possibility of interpreting monotheism as part of a general intellectual and ethical progress must be abandoned" (24). He argues forcefully and cogently against the evolutionary view: that monotheism

---

4. P. Radin, *Monotheism Among Primitive Peoples* (Basel: Ethnographical Museum, 1954; also issued as Special Publication No. 4 of the Bollingen Foundation).

emerges from, or is later or higher than, polytheism or animism (29–30).

Radin bases monotheism not upon developmental stages, but rather upon the idea of temperament. Some people everywhere are by temperament monotheistic; they have a monotheistic psychology. "All the monotheists, it is my claim, have sprung from the ranks of the eminently religious" (25). "Such people are admittedly few in number..." "It is the characteristic of such individuals, I contend, always to picture the world as a unified whole" (ibid.). These are the theological thinkers, a small elite in any culture, sharing a common temperament, and their influence upon their brethren in the same culture is stubborn and effective.

The inexpugnable persistence of monotheistic religion could be psychologically accounted for by Jung's theory of the self. Then we might be tempted to conclude that monotheism is so strong because it is the theological equivalent of a more complete, integrated, and powerful (numinous) psychic condition. But already two objections crop up. First, Radin says monotheism "has obviously not been the triumph of the unifying principle over the disruptive" (29). I take this to mean that religious and social order and disorder, unity and disunity cannot be correlated with monotheism and polytheism. Second, to base the strength of religious monotheism upon analogy with the psychologically more complete state of the self begs the same question, which is nowhere established: the superiority of monotheism to polytheism. Persistence does not necessarily demonstrate the superiority of monotheism, nor even its victory. Gray[5] points out

---

5. C. Buchanan Gray, *Hebrew Monotheism* (Oxford Society of Historical Theology, Abstract of Proceedings for the Year 1922–23), cited by Radin, *Monotheism*, 22. On the polytheism that existed side by side with Greek monotheism, see M. Nilsson, *Greek Piety*, trans. H. J. Rose (New York: Nor-

that two varying attitudes toward God can exist at one and the same time; the monolatry of Yahweh did exist among the Jews (even as late as the Exile period) side by side with the worship of other deities.

Despite the historical evidence of religions, there is a fond notion without adequate foundation that monotheism is the pinnacle and that "the evolution of religion thus manifests, it would seem, a definite tendency toward an integration of our mental and emotional life" (Radin, 6). Jung may not be borne out by the historical facts of religion, but he is borne out by the psychological bias of the historians of religion who put monotheism on top in the name of integration.

Two examples help to show this bias towards evolutionary monotheism. In his examination of the decline of Greek religion, Nilsson[6] finds the movement of religion from single, well-delineated gods to a multiplicity of powers and daimons a degeneration. The magic, superstition, and occultism that prevailed in later periods was, according to Nilsson (of Protestant Sweden), a disintegration. A century earlier, Schelling fantasied a vague *Urmonotheismus*, which developed later into a clearly formulated monotheism of the Old Testament as the highest product of religious consciousness. Between the first primitive monotheism and the later highly developed stage, there occurred Babel, which for Schelling represented the incursion of polytheism.

The hypothesis of the superiority of the self and monotheism over anima/animus and polytheism finds companions among

---

ton, 1969), 116–17 ("Monotheism"). Judeo-Christian monotheism in its conflict with Greek paganism, however, was tolerant of co-existence, cf. Nilsson, *Greek Piety*, 124.

6. M. Nilsson, "The Dionysiac Mysteries of the Hellenistic and Roman Age," in *Skrifter utgivna av Svenska Institutet i Athen*, vol. 5 (Lund: Gleerup, 1957). Cf. the last chapter of Nilsson's *Greek Piety*.

historians of religion. Consequently, Jung's hypothesis may be one more expression of the theological temperament. This temperament has been more narrowly described as introversion, for Jung writes: "The monistic tendency is a characteristic of introversion, the pluralistic of extraversion."[7] As in other areas of human activity, Jung sees the two tendencies in theology, where they are expressed as monotheism and polytheism, to be also "in constant warfare."[8] Neither of these two attitudinal tendencies is superior to the other and neither is an evolution of the other. They are givens and given as equals.

So, too, we must keep distinct the ideas of individual and of cultural development, the self stage of the individual and the monotheistic stage of religion. It is nowhere established (despite E. Neumann) that the stages of religious thought (if there are such things, and Radin doubts it) necessarily parallel stages of individual consciousness (if there are such things). Moreover, according to Radin, we should not think in developmental terms at all about the kinds of religion. Culture and religion do not move upwards from the many to the one, from disorder to order, from Babel to Jahweh: monotheism is not identical with superiority except from within its own *Anschauung*.

The idea of superior monotheism, and progressive stages toward it, has been instrumental to the notion of a superior self, attained through the progressive stages of individuation. Now since monotheistic superiority is questionable, so the superiority of monotheistic models for the self should as well be questioned.

Perhaps linear thinking in stages is but another reflection of a monotheistic temperament whose Judeo-Christian fantasies favor historical development and hierarchical improvement, whereas the anima/animus and its model of polytheism tend

---

7. *CW*6: 318.
8. *CW*5: 149.

toward a multiple field of circularity. Perhaps we should be less certain about stages of development in religion and in the individual and more questioning of the kind of consciousness that perceives in terms of stages.

Our argument has already turned psychological. We are no longer examining the religious evidence presented by Radin, but rather the psychological theory he proposes: that monotheism results from "an intellectual-religious expression of a very special type of temperament and emotion."

We have already suggested in these pages[9] last year which specific archetypal pattern tends to manifest in descriptions of the self. The self is personified as the Old Wise Man; its images are so often said to be ordering, e.g., geometric figures, crystals and stones, and abstractions beyond imagery; the behavior associated with the self and the process that leads to it is usually presented in the language of introversion, generic to "children of Saturn." From the viewpoint of an archetypal psychology "the special type of temperament and emotion" that produces monotheism and favors the self above anima/animus and views their relation in stages would be the senex. This archetype might also help account for theological monotheism's obdurate persistence, religious intolerance, and conviction of superiority. It might also account for the peculiarity of the self concept, which works symbolically to unite the realms of religion and of psychology into an indiscriminate whole. This leads to theological confusion about psychologizing God—a problem with which Jung was ever bothered. It leads also to psychological confusions about theologizing the psyche, producing dogmas, propitiatory rites,

---

9. J. Hillman, "On Senex Consciousness," *Spring: An Annual of Archetypal Psychology and Jungian Thought* (1970). Reprinted in *Senex & Puer*, The Uniform Edition of the Writings of James Hillman, vol. 3 (Putnam, Conn.: Spring Publications, 2005).

priesthoods, and worship. Likewise, the emphasis upon the self of psychological monotheism may help explain the theological interests of contemporary Jungians (as well as the Jungian interest of contemporary ministers) and the peculiar blending of analytical psychology with Christianity, which we shall discuss below as the "Protestant direction."

II

What then about polytheism and the anima/animus? Let us first suspend monotheism, both in our theological judgments and our psychological convictions about stages, about unity and about linear and even spiral advancement. Let us also try to suspend the pervasive influence of our monotheistic desires for a utopia of integration (Kronos's Golden Age), and that fantasy of individuation that characterizes it mainly as a movement towards the Old Wise Man and that, by subtly obscuring the differences between psychological man and theological man, prepares the ground, in Radin's language, for a monotheistic elite of "eminently religious individuals...admittedly few in number." By putting in suspension the senex domination of our attitudes, we might regard polytheism afresh and *psychologically*.

Jung used a polycentric description for the objective psyche. He envisioned it as a multiplicity of partial consciousness, like stars or sparks or luminous fishes' eyes.[10] Psychological polytheism corresponds with this description and provides its conceptual formulation in the traditional language of our civilization, i.e., classical mythology. By providing a divine background of personages and powers for each complex, it would find place for each spark. It would aim less at gathering them into a unity and

---

10. *CW* 8: 388ff.

more at integrating each fragment according to its own principle, giving each god its due over that portion of consciousness, that symptom, complex, fantasy, which calls for an archetypal background. It would accept the multiplicity of voices, the Babel of the anima and animus, without insisting upon unifying them into one figure, and accept, too, the dissolution process into diversity as equal in value to the coagulation process into unity. The pagan gods and goddesses would be restored to their psychological domain.

We would consider Artemis, Persephone, Athene, Aphrodite, for instance, as a more adequate *psychological* background to the complexity of human nature than the unified image of Maria, and the diversity expressed by Apollo, Hermes, Dionysus, and Hercules, for instance, to correspond better with psychological actualities than any single idea of self, or single figure of Eros, or of Jesus or Yahweh.

Focus upon the many and the different (rather than upon the one and the same) also provides a variety of ways of looking at one psychic condition. There are many avenues for discovering the virtues in a psychic phenomena. Depression, say, may be led into meaning on the model of Christ and his suffering and resurrection; it may through Saturn gain the depth of melancholy and inspiration, or through Apollo serve to release the blackbird of prophetic insight. From the perspective of Demeter depression may yield awareness of the mother-daughter mystery, or, through Dionysus, we may find depression a refuge from the excessive demands of the ruling will.

This emphasis upon many dominants would then favor the differentiation of the anima/animus. Quite possibly—and now this is my claim and contention—closer interest in a variety of divine hypostases and their processes displayed in myth will prove more psychological, even if less religious (in the monotheistic sense of religion). This interest will more likely produce more insights into emotions, images, and relationships, even if it be less encouraging for a theology of evolutional wholeness. It will more likely reflect accurately the illusions and entanglements of the soul, even if it satisfies less the popular vision of individuation from chaos to order, from multiplicity to unity, and where the health of wholeness has come to mean the one dominating the many.

Polytheistic psychology obliges consciousness to circulate among a field of powers. Each god has his due as each complex deserves its respect in its own right. In this circularity there seem no preferred positions, no sure statements about positive and negative, and therefore no need to rule out some events as "pathological." When the idea of progress through hierarchical stages is suspended, there will be more tolerance for the non-growth, non-upward, and non-ordered components of the psyche. There is more room for variance when there is more place given to variety. We may then discover that many of the judgments, which have previously been called psychological, were rather theological. They were statements about dreams and fantasies and behavior, and people too, coming from a monotheistic ideal of wholeness (the self).

Monotheism or polytheism, self or anima/animus pose still another either/or: theology or psychology. Traditionally, psychology deals with the second order of things, i.e., the emanated world of flux, diversity, and the phenomenally imperfect. Its concern has traditionally been with the actualities of the soul, its modes of existence, its fantasies, emotions, and experiences, whereas theology considers the soul eschatologically, from the viewpoint of self. Wholeness defined by psychology means everything—all the phenomena as phenomena, things as the present themselves. Wholeness defined theologically means the one—things as they are in God. From this difference can arise two views of completion, a psychological wholeness where individuation shows itself as being what one is as one is, and a theological wholeness where individuation shows itself in degrees of approximation to an ideal of unity. The more I am occupied by the anima or animus the more I will be concerned with the welter of psychological phenomena. The more I am occupied by the self, the more will I show concern with goal states, peak experiences, and universality.

From this superior vantage point, Babel and the proliferation of cults in the Hellenistic period always seem a degeneration. Likewise an "animus court" and its ambivalence, or the multiplicity of dream women, become but an inferior pre-stage of unity. (Remember how the Prophets warn against the promiscuity and harlotry of Israel.) The many-faceted world of Olympus must fade before a single God (even if in three persons).

But one might also consider the proliferation of cults as a *therapeia* (worship, service, and care) of the complexes in their many forms. Then one could understand the psychic fragmentation supposedly typical of our times as the return of the repressed, bringing a return of psychological polytheism. Fragmentation would then indicate many possibilities for individuation and might even be the result of individuation: each individual struggling with his *daimones*. If there is only one model of individuation can there be true individuality? The complexes that will not be integrated force recognition of their autonomous power. Their archetypal cores will not serve the single goal of monotheistic wholeness. Babel may be a religious decline from one point of view, but it may also be a psychological improvement, since through the many tongues complete psychic reality is being reflected. So the current delight in superstitions, witchery, and oracles have a psychological significance even if they be considered inferior religion. Through these images and practices anima/animus aspects of the psyche begin to find traditional reflection and containment in an impersonal background. Without the gods, who offer differentiated models for the peculiar psychic phenomena of anima and animus, we see them as projections. Then we try to take them back with introverted measures. But "the individual ego is much too small, its brain much too feeble, to incorporate all the projections withdrawn from the world. Ego and brain burst asunder in the effort; the psychiatrist calls it schizophrenia."[11] Without a consciously polytheistic psychology, are we not more susceptible to an unconscious fragmentation called schizophrenia?

Monotheistic psychology counters disintegration with archetypal images of order (mandalas). Unity compensates plurality. Polytheistic psychology would meet disintegration in its own language and archetypal likeness; there would be less need for compensation through opposites. The contrast between anima/animus and self appears in *Aion* as a contrast between pagan gods and the *imago Dei*. Of the anima/animus Jung writes:

> They are quite literally the father and mother of all the disastrous entanglements of fate and have long been recognized as such by the whole world. Together they form a divine pair, one of whom...is characterized by *pneuma* and *nous*, rather like Hermes with his ever-shifting hues, while the other...wears the features of Aphrodite, Helen (Selene), Persephone, and Hecate. Both of them are unconscious powers, "gods" in fact, as the ancient world quite rightly conceived them to be. To call them by this name is to give them that central position in the scale of values, which has always been theirs whether consciously acknowledged or not.[12]

The self of psychological wholeness, briefly, more clearly reflects the God of monotheism and the senex archetype.

---

11. *CW*11: 145.
12. *CW*9.2: 41.

Unity and totality stand at the highest point on the scale of objective values because their symbols can no longer be distinguished from the *imago Dei.* Hence all statements about the God-image apply also to the empirical symbols of totality. Experience shows that individual mandalas are symbols of *order,* and that they occur in patients principally during times of psychic disorientation or re-orientation. As magic circles they bind and subdue the lawless powers belonging to the world of darkness, and depict or create an order that transforms the chaos into a cosmos.[13]

Let me hasten to make clear that a polytheistic psychology is also religious. In following Jung we are regarding the anima and animus in their divine forms and are giving them "the central position in the scale of values that have always been theirs." Religion is not defined by the number of its gods but, rather, in terms of the observance or binding of events to one or many gods. Relating psychic events to many gods and many powers and *daimones* should not be assumed to a lessening of the glory of a single high God nor on the other hand a broadening of the single high God into something bigger and better. We can get away altogether from "better and worse" once we leave theological thinking and its monotheistic bias, which sets the question in that kind of language. Polytheistic psychology has room for the preferential enactment of any particular myth in a style of life. One may be Protestant, or Herculean, or Dionysian, or a melancholic child of Saturn, according to the archetypal core governing one's dominant complex, and thus one's fate. And even the myths may change in a life and the soul serve in its time many gods. Polytheistic psychology would not suspend the commandment to have "no other gods before me," but would extend

_____

13. Ibid.: 60.

that commandment for each mode of consciousness. Then, each archetypal possibility of the psyche—including those we now call psychopathological—could follow its principle of individuation within its particular divine model. No one model would be "before" another, since in polytheism the possibilities of existence are not jealous to the point of excluding each other. All are necessary that they together serve one law only: necessity. Polytheism gives archetypal psychology a religious mode even for psychopathology by suggesting an adequate background in myth for each of the sufferings of the soul.

III

The theme of monotheism/polytheism is immensely complex and packed with energy. The best minds of the early centuries of our era were obsessed with this issue and from that conflict of paganism with Christianity[14] our historical psyche and our psychological theory has been cast in what eventually became the current Protestant direction.

The essence of this direction reflects the Christian victory over the pagan world which can be summed up in a phrase from Gregory of Nazianzus who, while praising the pagans for their culture, epitomized the method for integrating it into Christianity: "We take prisoner every thought for Christ."[15] The one God swallows all the others; Pan was dead because monotheism had

14. *The Conflict between Paganism and Christianity in the Fourth Century*, ed. A. Momigliano (Oxford: Clarendon Press, 1963); see also E. R. Dodds, *Pagan and Christian in the Age of Anxiety* (Cambridge: At the University Press, 1965) for concise psychological characterization of the age and for references.

15. Gregory of Nazianzus, "In Praise of Basil" (*PG* 36, 508), quoted from J. Shiel, *Greek Thought and the Rise of Christianity* (New York: Barnes & Noble, 1968), 76. See further, B. Delfgaauw, "Gregor von Nazianz: Antikes und christliches Denken," *Eranos Yearbook* 36 (1967).

conquered. The variegated natural totality (Pan) of the pagan world's modes of being together with their attributes and traits and kinds of consciousness were taken prisoner through binding them to the one central image and myth. Monotheism fed like Kronos on the gods it swallowed. As Christianity swelled, imprisoned "Greek philosophy [read psychology] sank exhausted into the arms of religion."[16] Even were we to grant that this historical event was beneficial for religion—and there are others besides Nietzsche who would grudge any value to this victory—it was not necessarily beneficial for psychology. This because specific patterns of consciousness mimetic to various gods of the old pantheon were deprived of their archetypal backgrounds and imprisoned by the Christian model whose perspective now made them seem pathological. They could return but through the back door of mental aberration. A pathological view toward many of the psyche's phenomena is inevitable if psychology does not keep alive the totality of archetypal forms and their different ways of viewing the soul and life. Should psychology prefer instead to merge the many ways into a wholeness determined by monotheism, ego towards self, "single one to single One,"[17] will it not too—did it not already—sink exhausted into the arms of religion?

The Protestant direction of analytical psychology crops out in many large and small ways. Currently we see it in the emphasis

----

16. "Here knowledge is replaced by revelation in ecstasy. After Greek philosophy had performed this self-castration it sank exhausted into the arms of religion; as Proclus expresses in one of his hymns to the gods: 'And so let me anchor, weary one, in the haven of piety.'" E. Zeller, *Outlines of the History of Greek Philosophy*, trans. L.R. Palmer. (London: Kegan Paul, 1931), 313–15, quoted from J. Shiel, *Greek Thought and the Rise of Christianity*.

17. "This is the way to pray as single one to single one." Plotinus, *Enneads*, V, 1.6 (trans. Shiel), or "alone towards the alone" (trans. Mackenna). Cf. V, 9.11: "solitary to solitary."

upon love as a panacea, without differentiation of the faces of love and awareness of tradition in regard to its constellations; in the merit of hard work upon oneself; in the inculcation of a "strong ego" in therapy through the ennobling of choice, responsibility, commitment, and the consequent manipulation of guilt; in the trust in simplicity, naiveté, and group emotion; in an anti-intellectual, anti-logos bias where trust (*pistis*) in the "unconscious" or the "process" is enough; in an emphasis upon revelation (from dream, from oracle, imagination, psychosis, analyst, or from Jung); and in a peculiar combination of introverted religiosity and missionary popularization. We see it as well in the sole model for psychological suffering in which death's value is dislocated onto rebirth, linear process of gaining a better condition in exchange for a worse. This model fundamentally devalues the existential importance of depression and the descent into dissolution *per se*. Downward phenomena are good, not in themselves but rather because they offer hope for resurrection. It appears especially in the theological obsession with evil, which, let us recall, was not an issue in Greek polytheism. The Greeks had no Devil; each form of consciousness had its specific component of wrong-doing and tragedy. Evil was not a separate component but a strand so woven throughout everything that the "integration of the shadow" was already given in the patterns of life, rather than a task for an ego to do. And the Protestant direction appears in the notion of the "ego-self axis," the confrontation between them, the new midpoint as a new covenant, and "Christ as paradigm of the individuating ego."[18]

----

18. For basic formulations of the Protestant direction, see particularly the writings of E. Edinger: "Christ as Paradigm of the Individuating Ego," *Spring: An Annual of Archetypal Psychology and Jungian Thought* (1966); "The Ego-Self Paradox," *Journal of Analytical Psychology* 5, no. 1 (1960); and "Ralph Waldo Emerson: Naturalist of the Soul," *Spring: An Annual of Archetypal Psychology*

When our model of individuation is governed by monotheistic psychology in its Protestant direction, every fantasy becomes a prisoner for Christ. Every fantasy cannot help but find meaning in term of the one path, like the pilgrim on his progress towards integration. Even those that do not willingly fit in can be taken prisoner through the idea of a "pagan anima," a "chthonic animus," a "puer inflation," or the "problem of evil." These concepts bind psychic events to the dominant myth of the Protestant direction. Where once science, and then clinical pragmatics, were the enemies of the psyche, today the threat to the psyche's freedom of symbol-formation is nothing else than fading Christianity coming back in the guise of a theology of the Self to claim the soul for its own. Releasing the swallowed gods or the prisoners for Christ means realizing first how limited must be our hermeneutic for psychic phenomena when we have a monotheistic model for totality.

---

and Jungian Thought (1965), where we find (p. 97) the following passage: "In the process of assimilating the old culture to the new psychology, we discover again and again colleagues of the spirit. Emerson is such a colleague. He was a dedicated forerunner of the new world view that is only now beginning to reach its full emergence. The essence of this new view is well expressed by another colleague of the spirit, Teilhard de Chardin." The emphasis in both Emerson and Teilhard de Chardin is clearly upon a transcendental evolutionary wholeness. But Jung has been given many other kinds of spiritual colleagues. In textbooks he is grouped with Freud and Adler; in his own writings we find suggestions that he looks back upon a spiritual line that includes Goethe, Carus, Kerner, and the French alienists of the nineteenth century; that abrasive scandal to authority, Paracelsus, and Nietzsche too, can be colleagues of the spirit. Jung has also been placed alongside of Tillich and Buber, called the true successor of William James, and given for spiritual colleagues the Masters of the East, Albert Schweitzer, the Gnostics, and others too numerous and irrelevant to mention. The fact that there are these many views regarding Jung and his work is further witness to his multiple psychology and the multiplicity of viewpoints, i.e., polytheistic psychology, in general. The Protestant direction is only one ray in the spectrum.

Jung has pointed out that "the extermination of polytheism" goes hand in hand with the suppression of individual fantasy, and as "the Christian idea begins to fade, a recrudescence of individual symbol-formation may be expected."[19] We may draw the conclusion that "individual symbol-formation" requires a polytheistic psychology, because the symbols refer to their likenesses in the variety of archetypal forms through which they find their authentication. Did Jung foresee that his stress upon totality and wholeness could be turned by the influential monotheism of our culture and thus lead to a new onesidedness? The *imitatio Christi*, no longer a religious dogma or practice, becomes a psychological dogma subtly channeling the vital flow of individual fantasy back into the one old vessel, now called "wholeness."

Jung's contrast of the Christian with the polytheistic suggests a tension between them in his soul. In the tribute to Jung at his funeral, the minister spoke of Jung as a heretic. Jung's heresy, if we may follow his minister in calling it so, was however one of extension and revision, not of denial. He added a fourth to the trinity and therewith the dimension of psychic reality to Christian dogma. Therewith, too, the god within was re-affirmed. The experiential and phenomenological god of psychology included a fourth dimension, the underside of shadow, femininity, and the pagan past. He added to the Christ of orthodoxy the wealth of alchemical imagery, and like the Christian philosophers of earlier ages he connected his explorations again and again with the Christ image. Moreover, his description of the *imago Dei* as the Self follows the monotheistic model, by subsuming the many opposites under the highest goal, union. Sharper heresy was avoided.

---

19. *CW* 8: 92.

The East[20] (where the self notion, the mandala and the Old
Wise Man image are first at home) and alchemy provided ways
around the desperate issue of heresy, which so obsessed the
Renaissance giants and the more profound of the Romantics.
Bruno, who posited a plurality of worlds, was forced out of the
Dominican order and later burned; Ficino took another tack and
in his mid-life was ordained into the Church's service. Words-
worth's mystical pantheism declined into woolly support of
established religion. Coleridge, immersed fully in the dilemmas
of Neoplatonist polytheism (appearing in his day as pantheism),
"regarded himself as an orthodox Church of England man."[21]
The tension between his imaginal, sensuous life and his Christian convictions was said to have been at the core of Coleridge's
private agony. Blake followed the method of Gregory Nazianzus
by taking every fantasy into the Judea-Christian nexus. Those
who started boldly into paganism—Shelley, Keats, Byron—died
before the issue was fully upon them. Nikolai Berdyaev believed
the issue insoluble.[22]

Is this also true in the realm of psychology? Is the restoration of the pagan figures to their place as archetypal dominants of the psyche impossible in a monotheistic psychological
world? If so, then we must abandon our attempts at an archetypal approach based on polycentricity and accept analytical
psychology a prisoner for monotheism in its current Protestant direction and let psychology sink exhausted where it may.

------

20. For one instance of the Eastern reinforcement of monotheistic psychology see Jung's "Psychological Commentary on 'The Tibetan Book of the
Great Liberation,'" *CW*11: 798, beginning: "'There being really no duality,
pluralism is untrue.' This is certainly one of the most fundamental truths
of the East."

21. T. McFarland, *Coleridge and the Pantheist Tradition* (Oxford: Clarendon Press, 1969), 220; see further, 223.

22. Cf. his *The Meaning of the Creative Act* (New York: Charles Scribner's
Sons, 1936).

The task of psychology, let us stress, is not the reconciliation of monotheism and polytheism. Whether the many are each aspects of the one, or emanations of the one or its hypostases and persons is discussion for theology, not psychology. So, too, attempts to integrate the anima/animus into the self (as, for instance, the notion of stages) tend also to be theological: they present theories in the senex mode for integrating differences into a single order. The result generally disfavors the plurality of individual differences.

The way out of this dilemma is perhaps less theoretical than empirical. Which pattern offers my psyche in the mess of its complexes better options for meaning? Heuristic pragmatic criteria have always been decisive in choosing between rival structures of consciousness. Constantine became Christian (and through him our civilization) because the new monotheistic religion then offered redemption to lost areas of his psyche, which the paganism of the time could not quicken:[23] "The pagan cults were nothing but a confused medley, very loosely bound together by the customary dedication to 'all gods.' They had no common organization and tended to break up into their atoms."[24] The independence of the Greek city states and of the Renaissance Italian cities, the cry of liberty in the name of paganism during the Romantic Revolution, as well as the contemporary separatist movements show on the political level a psychological dissociation away from central authority. Translating these polytheistic and separatist phenomena into a psychological metaphor we have Jung's vision of the objective psyche where the atoms reflect the multiple sparks.

---

23. A. Alföldi, *The Conversion of Constantine and Pagan Rome*, trans. H. Mattingly (Oxford: Clarendon Press, 1948), 8.

24. Ibid., 12, where the presentation of the Christian victory over paganism is put altogether as a conquest by monotheism over polytheism.

Monotheism evidently provided Constantine's psyche with the central focus then needed. Today, may not the situation be the reverse? Can the atomism of our psychic paganism, that is, the rash of individual symbol formation now breaking out as the Christian cult fades, be contained by a psychology of self-integration that echoes its expiring Christian model? If so, then indeed, the self is "the archetype which it is most important for modern man to understand." The answer hangs in the historical balance; and the scale, so loaded with recrudescent individual fantasies, is surely tipping away from monotheism's definition of order and its *imago Dei*. The danger is that a true revival of paganism as *religion* is then possible, with all its accouterments of popular soothsaying, quick priesthoods, astrological divination, extravagant practices, and the erosion of psychic differentiations through delusional enthusiasms. The self does not provide bulwark, since its monotheistic description and protestant interpretation leave too much out. But when the self can be re-imagined through a variety of ambiguous archetypal perspectives and less assuredly through the senex, consciousness can find containers for its individual symbol formations. To meet the revival of paganism as religion we need adequate psychological models that give full credit to the psyche's inherent polytheism, thereby providing *psychological vessels* for the sparks. They may burst into religious conflagrations when left psychologically unattended or when forced into monotheistic integrations that simply do not work.

The restoration of the gods and goddesses as psychic dominants reflects truly both the varied beauty and messy confusion, and tragic limitation, of the anima/animus, their fascinating multiplicity, their conflicts, their lack of ethical cohesion, their tendency to draw us deep through life and into death. Polytheistic psychology can give sacred differentiation to our psychic turmoil and can welcome its outlandish individuality in terms of classical patterns.

The elaboration of these patterns in psychological terms is yet to be done. We have still to understand Artemis and Persephone, Apollo and Poseidon, in terms of our soul-images and behavior. Although Jung did devote much space in his works to the divine couple and their configurations, and also to the personal aspects of the anima and animus in our lives, he concentrated mainly upon the phenomenology of the self archetype. The same thorough work needs to be done upon the anima/animus. But before this work can be done we would have to recognize their importance and see things from within their archetypal perspective, i.e., in terms of a polytheistic psychology. Hence, the urging in these remarks. The idea of four stages[25] of the anima and animus, inspired mainly from Goethe and where progression moves away from the physical and toward the spiritual, is only an initial attempt at an anima/animus phenomenology in terms of classical mythology. Until we follow Jung in examining the differentiation of wholeness with the same care that he applied to the integration of wholeness, our psychology does not meet the psyche's need for archetypal understanding of its problems.

If there are other psychological options for our need I cannot find them. These ideas and their presentation leaves much unsatisfied, and so others who may see the question and its answers more clearly are invited to respond to this issue along lines laid out here.

---

25. On the four levels of the anima, see *CW*16: 361; on the four levels of the animus, taken from Faust, see E. Jung, *Animus and Anima* (Putnam, Conn.: Spring Publications, 2008), 8–9. For an elaboration of the anima in terms of the Greek Kore figure, see *CW*9.1: 306–83.

POSTSCRIPT (1981)

So concluded the original paper published ten years ago. It was followed by ten responses—notably that of Kathleen Raine on Blake's Christian polytheism.[26] Then, in October 1976, at meetings of the American Academy of Religion in St. Louis, there were another ten discussants of the theme monotheism/polytheism. Both David L. Miller and I were engaged in this panel, together with Elizabeth Sewell, Richard Underwood, Tom Moore, William Paden, Daniel Noel, and others. These responses attempted to clarify errors of thinking—philosophical, historical, theological. The psychological issue remained pretty well avoided. Once more, in 1979, when a revised version of the article appeared in German in *Gorgo*,[27] it was followed by comments of which those of Wolfgang Giegerich and Ulrich Mann especially stand out.

These discussions made clear the need to emend (not amend). Some of this has already been done in subsequent essays. That is, the concern of this 1971 piece was articulated in detail in my 1972 Terry Lectures[28] and in my "Anima" articles in *Spring* (1973 and 1974).[29] This piece has been a groundwork for what came later, as David L. Miller was the first to espy. Though emendations are still needed, I cannot possibly encompass in this postscript all the issues raised by the discussants nor give them due justice. I

---

26. G. Adler, T. Cowan, R. López-Pedraza, K. Raine, J.M. Spiegelman, et. al., "Responses and Contributions," *Spring: An Annual of Archetypal Psychology and Jungian Thought* (1971): 209–32.

27. "Die Psychologie: monotheistisch oder polytheistisch," *Gorgo: Zeitschrift für archetypische Psychologie und bildhaftes Denken* 1 (1979): 1–21.

28. J. Hillman, *Re-Visioning Psychology* (New York: Harper & Row, 1975).

29. "Anima," *Spring: An Annual of Archetypal Psychology and Jungian Thought* (1973): 97–132; "Anima II," *Spring: An Annual of Archetypal Psychology and Jungian Thought* (1974): 113–46.

don't even want to try. I just want to use this ring to get in one or two more licks.

1. What I have suggested as a polytheistic psychology has inescapably been taken as a polytheistic theology whose target is Christianity and Judeo-Christian monotheism. The psychological issue here is not whether that was or is my aim, disguised or plain, but rather *can one do psychology without at the same time doing theology*? In 1971, Philipp Wolff's response said that this was precisely the dilemma of Jungian psychology: it uses religious categories for describing the psychic world and hence is willy-nilly entangled in theology. He is right. The Jungian context of this piece is nowhere more visible than in the deliberate interpenetration of psychology and theology. Jung's psychology always has theological implications and where it was often ignored by psychiatrists it was vividly, even rabidly, engaged with by theologians. The collaboration in this book of Miller's, between him, Corbin, and myself exhibits the interpenetration of theology and a psychology of soul. If we want to move psychology and therapy we have to move its baggage too.

And no baggage more weighs down our every psychological step than the monotheism of our culture, which, because the culture has slid into secularism, no longer appears with the devout and fanatic visibility of Islam; instead monotheism appears in hundreds of inevitable psychological presuppositions about how things are and how they should be. *E pluribus unum* is only a tiny manifestation of the ubiquity of singleness whose ultimate magnifico is the Western Ego, monotheism wholly subjectivized and reduced to secular humanistic psychology. Miller's excellent new Introduction showing the contemporary rise of plurals nevertheless assumes as background a vast, louring, and tacit monotheism against which these plurals seem mere cries and whispers.

Because the opposition of monotheism to polytheism is so much the baggage of the culture, it is deep in the collective unconscious of each of us. Whatever we say, whatever we write, is so packed with monotheistic assumptions, that an understanding of the polytheistic psyche is almost impossible. Never mind that a pagan Renaissance, as Berdyaev said above, is forever impossible in a Christian world: what is more seriously impossible, because so unconscious, is simply an understanding of our cultural foundations—Homer, Plato, Aristophanes, Plotinus—because we approach the polytheistic world freighted with monotheistic baggage. That we still call "pagan" what in fact is classic and the very soil of our mythical imagination is a piece of that baggage. Even the Christian texts used to back up its viewpoint have narrowed to such singleness of meaning that their rich classical echoes are lost. Take *singleness* itself. Matthew 6:22 (cf. Luke 11:34): "if therefore thine eye be single, thy whole body shall be full of light." Single (*haplous*) means open, plain, frank, natural, downright, straightforward and simple. But now that the word single only means univocal, monocular singleness, the passage itself will be read in a puritan and fundamentalist manner, demonstrating that inherent tendency within monotheistic consciousness to take its rhetoric with singleness of meaning, i.e., literally. When the One means "only" (one-ness, one-sidedness), literalism is inevitable.

It hardly matters to me whether theology or psychology brings awareness to our baggage as long as awareness comes. Rather than separating the theo-psychic mixture, let it continue. It will any how. It's an authentic compound, for the soul itself is just this sort of mixture. By definition soul has a religious concern and is naturally involved with theological questions. We can no more leave that concern and those questions to professional theologians (staggering under their suitcases) than could C.G. Jung.

2. Of course, this welcoming of theology leaves polytheistic psychology open to theological corrections such as were brought by colleagues from Religion at St. Louis and again most intelligently by Ulrich Mann in *Gorgo*. For instance: how can we assume that Christianity is fading; have I not missed the piety and probity of the very Protestant direction I attack; and have I not simplified the beautiful complexity, mystery, and (inherent polytheistic) wealth of Christian monotheism? Most important, however, have I not been promulgating a religious ground to psychology which then leaves it short by not following through with the elaboration of praxis: cult, rite, prayer, sacrifice, and community. And what about belief?

As I have spelled out in several later writings, *psychological* polytheism is concerned less with worship than with attitudes, with the way we see things and place them. Gods, for psychology, are neither believed in nor addressed directly. They are rather adjectival than substantive; the polytheistic experience finds existence qualified with archetypal presence and recognizes faces of the Gods in these qualifications. Only when these qualities are literalized, set apart as substances, that is, become theologized, do we have to imagine them through the category of belief.

Do polytheistic cultures have a category of belief like ours, with credal disputes and credal affiliations? Egyptians and Polynesians, Peruvians and Mesopotamians, Greeks and Hindus and Celts—did they, do they take doctrinal oaths, make theological statements in order to belong, in order to experience their Gods? Let's steer clear of belief,just like the Greeks. As Tom Moore pointed out, myths are read with humor, not belief. The gods don't require my belief for their existence, nor do I require belief for my experience of their existence. It's enough to know I am mortal to feel their shadowing. It's enough just to look around with open eyes. Belief helps only when one can't see, or must see through a glass, darkly. Faith as I think of it is an animal faith (Santayana): what is there is there and not because I believe it, nor will it go away when I stop believing. The dog who sniffs the wind doesn't believe in the wind: he simply tries to pick up on it and get what it is saying. Not so simple, by the way.

Psychology can do very well without the category of belief. We will still go on dreaming, even if we "don't believe in dreams" and we will still go on loving and hating and struggling with our *daimones,* whether we declare belief in them or not. Belief leads us into so many of the old alleys, closed in by walls: subjectivism; evidence; the status of the "objects of belief"; delusion, illusion, and belief; the problem of doubt and all those guilty torments. Merely by letting go of this one bag, how straightly, easily we walk into the wind.

There is another reason not to follow through with prescriptions for religious practices. Maybe cult, rite, sacrifice, prayer, and community are already going on—if we look at psychotherapy with a religious eye. Maybe a sort of polytheistic religion-propitiation of *daimones,* active engagements with images of imagination, creative dialogue (one of Corbin's definitions of prayer), is already being practiced in the communities around the consulting room. It wouldn't be too forced to use the metaphors of religion when looking at what goes on in psychotherapy. And then we would not be so obliged to be literally religious, that is, devise and proscribe practices that are not necessary if one sees what is already taking place with a religious eye. And it is this eye, not the promulgation of a New Church of Polytheism, that my article and David Miller's *The New Polytheism* is all about.

3. We would have been spared these sorts of debate had the 1971 article not been cast in debate form. Its rhetoric of conceptual

argument (mono *or* poly) remains monotheistic in spite of itself. This shows again the difficulty of trying to enter the polytheistic mode of consciousness after Pan is dead. We are forced to fire up old Hellenistic and Patristic thought patterns: whose system is better, yours or mine. Psychology vanishes in that steam. We are left with the monotheistic conundrums of dualism.

These appeared in the discussions. Spiegelman used a Kundalini model of many centers, no single one of which had supreme authority. However, the one remains invisibly as the energy flowing within the system as a unified whole, so that essentially the many are contained by and expressions of the one. Cowan paradoxically blended one and many by means of the Greek word Pan, which means both "all" and "every." But Pan is dead, and didn't he die and that paradox split at that time in antiquity when the new God of Christian monotheism appeared ending the possibility of the Greek resolution Cowan proposes? Kathleen Raine gave our dualism another dimension: spirit and soul, spiritual monotheism and psychological polytheism. But, here Radin's caution must be recalled: monotheism sets itself higher than polytheism. In *Gorgo*, Giegerich turned it the other way. Monotheism is a narrowed and extremest partial truth, while polytheism is higher because it is more basic, ubiquitous, and lasting.

So, I prefer López-Pedraza's formulation: "The many contains the unity of the one without losing the possibilities of the many." This restates the Neoplatonist idea of *skopos*: the thematic unity of intention, the aim or target that gives an internal necessity and fittingness to each part of a work of art. Here, the one is not something apart and opposed to the many, leaving them as inchoate fragmented bits, but it appears as the unity of each thing, that it is as it is, with a name and a face.

As a psychic reality, the one appears only as this or that image: a voice, a number, a whirlwind, a universal idea, etc. And, it appears as the unity of each particular event, discoverable phenomenally only within eachness. The arguments that the one is ground of the many, their continuity, or the whole that embraces them all are again biases of monotheistic consciousness attempting to usurp a more ultimate, more basic and superior place in a metapsychological system, where system itself belongs to *senex* rhetoric. We must watch out for words like "ground," and "whole," and "all," and remember that unity, too, can be imagined polytheistically. To polytheistic consciousness, the one does not appear as such but is contained as one among many and within each of the many, as López-Pedraza says. Corbin's prefatory letter above, and his Eranos essay on the paradoxes of monotheism,[30] can carry the reader deeper into the bewildering dualisms of monotheism.

This helps us remember that dualism is a function of monism. Arguments between "the One and the Many" play themselves out in an arena already set up by monotheistic consciousness. Pluralism, however, is a wholly different kettle of fish, which gets emptied out when put into the dualistic framework of the One versus the Many, as if, as some discussants indicated, this is really what the whole game of monopoly comes down to. Philosophy enjoys these games, these reductions often considering all questions ultimately to be footnotes to Plato (e.g., the One/Many eristics in the *Parmenides*). Where philosophy literally means Plato, psychology is more interested in the footnotes, the *midrashim* below the line. That's where the deviations and twists are, and that's where it gets under your skin.

––––––––––––

30. "Le paradoxe du monothéisme," *Eranos-Yearbook* 45 (1976): 6–133.

For example: the connections made by López-Pedraza[31] between classical polytheism and Freud's polymorphous sexuality puts the Problem of the Many in a freshly threatening manner. Polytheism becomes polysexuality, no longer merely for philosophers, but a host of devils in our own backyard of desire. Another example: that Pan and Priapus, Dionysos, Hermes, Aphrodite and Ares are gods and goddesses means that the images, fantasies, and behaviors they offer us—all the obscenity, riot, trickery, and war—are divine, backed by divinity, with an *ethos* and a *logos*. What a radical revolution in our philosophical surety about good and bad, right and wrong, sick and well. No wonder philosophy has to defend itself against this radicality (root-going, rooted) with terms such as "relativism."

What monotheistic consciousness sees only as radical relativism is from a polytheistic point of view radical facticity: for there is no need to put it all together. That need is itself a fantasy or a paranoid drive toward unified meaning that has not been seen through to its archetypal base in what I called above, the *senex*. It can be argued that the polytheistic hypothesis "puts it all together" even if ina different way: at least it gives a coherent account. True; but also not true, because there is no "polytheistic hypothesis" when within its perspective. There is merely the method of *epistrophē* and a consistent attitude, but no attempt at overall coherence. Henri Frankfort explains it like this:

> The ancients did not attempt to solve the ultimate problems confronting man by a single and coherent theory... Ancient thought—mythopoeic, "myth-making" thought— admitted side by side certain *limited* insights, which were held to be *simultaneously* valid, each in its own proper context, each corresponding to a definite avenue of approach.

---

31. R. López-Pedraza, *Hermes and His Children* (Zurich: Spring Publications, 1977), 67.

I have called this "multiplicity of approaches"... this habit of
thought agrees with the basic experience of polytheism.[32]

The dualism with monotheism is one way philosophy holds
polytheism in tandem. Philosophical rhetoric works with com-
parison, antinomies, the law of contradiction. It pairs darkness
with light, whereas a poem can shade in qualities of darknesses
("Thirteen Ways of Looking at a Blackbird") without reference
to light, and a painting can differentiate any topos without having to contrast it with another. Polytheism is not necessarily
half of a philosophical pair, requiring monotheism for its other
side. In itself, polytheism is a style of consciousness—and this
style should not even be called "polytheistic," for strictly, historically, when polytheism reigns there is no such word. Where the
daimones are alive, "polytheism," "pantheism," "animism," and
even "religion" do not appear. The Greeks had daimones but not
these terms, so we ought to hold from using monotheistic rhetoric when entering that imaginative field and style we have been
forced to call "polytheistic."

Then we might better discover this other psychological eye
by imagistic, mythic, and poetic means, releasing intuitive insights from sensate particular events. The psyche, and the
world's psyche, too, would show its patterns in tales and images
and the physiognomic qualities of things. The whole show would
be different, and indeed psychic life is show, both the comedy
and agony of drama, and Schau, each appearance an imagistic
essence, a showing forth; revelations, theophanies.

When William James described A Pluralistic Universe,[33] he set
this sentence in italics: "Reality MAY exist in distributive form, in

---

32. H. Frankfort, Ancient Egyptian Religion: An Interpretation (New York:
Columbia University Press, 1948), 4.

33. Essays in Radical Empiricism and A Pluralistic Universe (New York:
E. P. Dutton, 1971), 183.

the shape not of an all but of a set of eaches, just as it seems to be."
Then he added: "There is this in favor of eaches, that they are at
any rate real enough to have made themselves at least appear to
everyone, whereas the absolute [wholeness, unity, the one] has
as yet appeared immediately to only a few mystics, and indeed to
them very ambiguously."

Eachness: that is the place I share with James—and with Jung,
for what else is individuation but a particularization of the soul.
For James, eachness is not so much achieved through an individuating process as it is already there "just as it seems to be."James
plays his eachness on a Blue Guitar, "things as they are," the blue
bush of imagination inextricably embedded in the plain sense
of things. Only with these individual eaches can we be intimate,
says James. The pluralist vision opens toward intimacy, love, and
the immediate green world of the senses. O taste and see! As Jung
said, the archetypes cannot be understood without the feeling
function. Psychic life is particularized in the vale of the world,
and this vale is endlessly alive with qualities, an embeddedness
(Whitehead) of concretely felt individualities which are not, no,
not at all, sufficiently described as the Ten-Thousand Things,
atomic particles, plurality, the Many, or by any of the other terms
of perception theory, physics' theory, or religious doctrine enun-
ciated by a detached monotheistic consciousness that sits in
judgement so far above the vale that it seems only unqualified
statistical data, a blooming buzzing confusion of quanta, face-
less and threatening.

Here, within and below, we are embedded in immediate con-
texts and the idea of the Many only serves to sever us, and
the strings of the guitar. The Many is a defensive idea against
the experiences of things as they are. That hat you're wear-
ing, the pain in your eyes, my last dream this morning, the dog
scratching her collar. Each image holds itself together. Gone the

fragments, the bits, and so gone, too, are the needs for a unified world view and a unified personality to uphold the world, and a Self to hold it all. Each event showing its own face is the way the world comes and our lives are, and these events have a *kami* (Japanese), a *theos* (Greek), bespeaking the holiness of things as images of gods.

Too quickly we monotheize this "images of gods"; as if the images were one-to-one representations, mirror images of actual gods we admire in museum statuary. As if we had to match each *ness* with its multiple background. No; myth-matching is only an eye exercise: we must look for mythic images in order to see imagistically. Once the imagistic mode is in the eye, then the phrase "as images of gods" is less literal and instead refers to a theophanic kind of consciousness where psychic reality is omni-present; no palpable distinction between soul and vale of-the-world, *anima mundi*.

This last leads to another, an aesthetic, sense of life, to poly-theistic psychology as an aesthetic psychology. But that must be left for another time, even if adumbrations are already here in this piece. For, an aesthetic psychology derives from a world ensouled whose qualities are given directly as physiognomic affordances with the nature of each event in its interplay with others. All things signed, signifying; a calligraphy of inherent intelligibility. And this language, we already know in our ani-mal souls.

4. I have spent so many words on theological and philosophical aspects because this is a postscript to an addendum in a book by a professor of religions. The book's concern is a theological revi-sion. Still, my concern is more the re-visioning of *psychotherapy*. A polytheistic model of the psyche seems logical and helpful when confronting the many voices and figments that pop up in any single patient, including myself. I can't even imagine how we

could ever have got on in therapy without a polytheistic background. For a long time I was not able to understand why clinicians had such an investment in the strong ego, the suppressive integration of personality, and the unified independence of will at the expense of ambivalence, partial drives, complexes, imagos, vicissitudes—to say nothing of hallucinations and split personality—until I heard sounding through this clinical language the ancient and powerful *basso profundo* of the One. Clinical rhetoric has been so persuasive (especially when lent a helping hand and brass knuckles by clinical pharmacology and the legal system) because it speaks with the superior rhetoric, that rhetoric of superiority, of monotheistic consciousness. In clinical situations, this consciousness reinforces the notion of the 'I' (*le moi, das Ich*) and then what else can the gods do but become diseases, which is where Jung found them.

This is also where William James found his plurals, his eaches. I refer to the very same passage (p. 268), which Miller quotes in opening his introduction. James's view rises from "analogies with ordinary psychology and with the facts of pathology, with those of psychical research...and religious experience." Or what he also calls there: "the particular, the personal, and the unwholesome."

How sorry, how sick, literally, that we get to this style of consciousness only through "the facts of pathology and psychical research." But this is our monotheistic culture. As James Frazer wrote:

> the divisibility of life, or...the plurality of souls, is an idea suggested by many familiar facts, and has commended itself to philosophers like Plato as well as to savages. It is only when the notion of a soul...becomes a theological dogma that its unity and indivisibility are insisted upon as essential. The savage, unshackled by dogma, is free to

> explain the facts of life by the assumption of as many souls
> as he thinks necessary.[34]

What a different experience of breakdown and clinic emerges when, unshackled by dogma, we may assume as many souls as necessary. Is not this very dogma what has made these souls "sick"? Has not this dogma made the world soul in our civilization sick by turning it away from the facts of life, things as they are, our savage selves?

Perhaps the clinical re-visioning I have been struggling with ever since I entered into an analysis of my own piece of that sickness, and then repeatedly in writings since 1960, does find its logos in the polytheistic premise of this article which works, by means of old fashioned disputations, to release the divine soul figures, anima and animus, from the dogma of self domination. Therapy of the individual and of the *anima mundi* proceed apace. Clinical re-visioning is simultaneously revolution of *Weltanschauung.* To quote Frankfort again:

> Polytheism is sustained by man's experience of a universe
> alive from end to end. Powers confront man wherever he
> moves, and in the immediacy of these confrontations the
> question of their ultimate unity does not arise.[35]

By suspending the question of ultimate unity we may become like those savages, sylvan, animals in the woods, tracing our paths according to impinging necessities and the presence of powers. And this savage is not a rough beast slouching—or is only so, if Bethlehem be the capital word in the last line. That beast has been savaged by the same dogma; our conversion perverting him into the wild man whose return we fear, unable to distinguish the second coming from the return of the repressed.

---

34. *The Golden Bough,* abbr. ed., (New York: Macmillan, 1947), 690.
35. Frankfort, *Ancient Egyptian Religion,* 4.

Nor is the savage Rousseau's, although deep in that nostalgia are the stirrings of Pan, the only animal-haunched god in the Greek pantheon. Pan has fled nature's arcadia. All the gods are within. So now he resides in the wild imagination, its caves, its chases, its natural freedom to form as it pleases, the "recrudescence of individual symbol-formation" that Jung, above, says may be expected "as the Christian idea begins to fade." Maybe Pan is not altogether dead, nor Julian either, nor Celsus's pages wholly burnt; and if polemical strife is the father of each and every event, maybe this appendix whose eristics attempt to constellate Eris, demon of strife, will continue to father new psychic life by rehearsing in our day once more the ancient claim of polytheism.

Made in the USA
Las Vegas, NV
01 November 2022

58533624R00090